The Shadow of My Life

The Shadow of My Life

HOPE CHANCE

LitPrime Solutions
21250 Hawthorne Blvd
Suite 500, Torrance, CA 90503
www.litprime.com
Phone: 1 (209) 788-3500

© 2020 Mary Dell Sharp. All rights reserved.

No part of this book may be reproduced, stored in a retrieval system, or transmitted by any means without the written permission of the author.

Published by LitPrime Solutions   12/19/2020

ISBN: 978-1-953397-46-1 (sc)
ISBN: 978-1-953397-47-8 (e)

Any people depicted in stock imagery provided by Thinkstock are models, and such images are being used for illustrative purposes only.

Certain stock imagery © Thinkstock.

Because of the dynamic nature of the Internet, any web addresses or links contained in this book may have changed since publication and may no longer be valid. The views expressed in this work are solely those of the author and do not necessarily reflect the views of the publisher, and the publisher hereby disclaims any responsibility for them.

I want to thank my publisher, LitPrime for undying faith in my book. They stood behind me all the way never faultering one step behind but forging ahead without doubt or hesitation and I thank them for that.

This is my story and it is not pretty, my true friend of 40 years and my other friend of 25 years never faultered nor doubted me. They were there every step of the way as was my publisher. My book reminds me of the poem

The Invictus...

It matters not how strait the gate,
How charged with punishments the scroll,
I am the master of my fate,
I am the captain of my soul.

And so it is The Shadow of My Life, the light is now brighter than one could possibly imagine.

God is so good in ways that are unimaginable.
Thanks again LitPrime
Hope Chance

*This is dedicated to Fr Tom believing in me
When I didn't believe in myself*

Contents

Foreword xi

School Of Fine Art Of Drama 1
The Folks I Met At The School 4
Our Hangout Between Classes And Afterwards 7
The Season's End 9
Beginning Of The End 12
Good-Bye 15
Time To Start Over 23
Home For The Weekends .25
Fatal Decision 28
Decision Made 32
Back To The Midwest 36
Possibly Leveling Off Maybe? 41
Settled Down In Smalltown Purchased A House 45
Saundra Shows Abnormal Hateful Behavior 46
Sometimes It Was A Reality Othertimes Insanity 48
Home Became City 50
And So The Interview Starts 52
The D Word 54
The Temporary Moving Day 59
On The Lamb For 6 Weeks 60

The Next Huge Wave, The Divorce Itself 65
Now The Games Begin 67
Finding A New Home 70
Really, The End Of The Story? You Have To Be Kidding 73
Peroid Of Adjustment 76
Relocation One More Time 82
Could This Be Some Kind Of Sign? 83
Travelin Buddies 90
Dare I Relocate One More Time? 94
Insurance, To Grease And Oil Company, On To Aarc
    National Office 101
Private Investigator 107
This Thing Called Life 113

Foreword

This book has been written to share many life changing events that are truly proof that for every door that closes another opens.

I have shared my doors. There is absolutely nothing that we cannot overcome if we indeed put our mind to it. My entire life is living proof of this.

We are always taught "God is with us, He is there" and we immediately put that teaching in the back of our minds and there it sits never to be thought of again. Later in time of need, we say "exactly where is He in all this?" My life is fact after fact. He is there, always, we only have to look around. If one reads my book you can certainly see that is very true "When He shuts one door, even with a hard slam, another door does in fact open"

What you will read is not a victim's story, no way, it is that of a winner who is enjoying the "winter of her life"

God Bless You, Live, love and be happy, above all **BELIEVE!**

School Of Fine Art Of Drama

It is amazing now that I am in the winter of my years I notice that it seems morals are no more, the work place is not like it used to be, and values have switched to something I don't recognize in the most remote setting. It is amazing. I have seen a lot and lived a life of interesting situations that even I can't imagine happened to me.

This book is life, love and survival in a world I didn't want to be in.

I do not use my real name in writing this that cannot happen in this lifetime anyway. The life I have lived through is one most would not have survived and even now I have to shudder when I think back. This is being written in hopes others will realize whatever the situation they are in … it will pass and is actually only a small "byte" of time.

I was raised by the old school of values. I was taught to have high morals, work and work hard, be honest, respect and love your family. Yes all these are the old time values that are where I am from.

I went to grade school, graduated from high school as we all did (except the drifters as they were called then} Went to College, was in summer stock in my home town and from there to a professional drama school This was the ripe old age of 18 when I walked out on stage at the School of the Fine Art of Drama. My life was amazing. I was going to a professional drama school and worked hard very hard.

It was only a two year school so we had to work really hard. We didn't have vacations like other schools or colleges it was more like a 24 hour store which was just fine with me that is what I wanted all I could handle daily.

The school itself had five theatres all active. Daily rehearsals and openings we had been casted in two shows sometimes which made things hectic to rehearse two shows and also perform opening night two different theatres. Very much a challenge and it was pure heaven or I thought so at any rate.

The school itself was wonderful ; however, surprisingly not to teach you how to act. No, it was not for that purpose. Drama or Comedy they would find your peak and go from there. It was professional all the way. This was extremely hard work.

I did not go to the School to be taught how to act but rather to hone what skills I had to perfection which I did with lots of hard training. And, yes, the best teachers in the business.

I was never interested in the TV shows at all or movies I wanted the legitimate stage always. I was never involved with wanting to be a star I wanted to be a good actress that was my goal, always. I was using the School for the day I would be good enough for the East coast and that day would most definitely come. I could see it looming in the future. Every day it was closer and closer and I worked all that much harder.

What were the classes and exercises we went through daily? One hour of modern dance, ballet and fencing which was three hours in all? That was daily we also studied the costumes and worked hard with our speech, so we immediately dropped our flat A being from the midwest into what is called perfect standard stage speech which I still do today automatically. Our speech teacher was the best in the business. He taught many of the stars how to speak correctly there was no more mumbling. He was a brilliant man truly that is enough about the school that should be a book in itself. This school was amazing we had fantastic teachers. Our fencing teacher was a world renowned fencing champion the absolute best. He held the title of being the best fencer in the world. Of course our speech teacher and also working through studios on the west coast with their accents when warranted and just perfect stage speech, a broadway chirographer, and professional make up artist. Our directors were all well known clear across the United States with the highest credentials that was possible to have.

The Folks I Met At The School

I met some great people there. The school itself was small the attendance was only 75 so we all knew each other. We had some wonderful wonderful times. We loved to poke fun at each other and did so quite often. One time we decided to go horseback riding. Now mind you I am not what one would call a rider but I do stay in the saddle somehow. Dad taught me how to ride like many other things. We were all going to ride that day it was a beautiful day and there wasn't much smog that particular day so we took off riding around in a park looking at the scenery enjoying the ride and laughing a lot as kids do. Suddenly we realized we were on a highway that was not open. The concrete was still wet. We all looked at each other and decided to get the hell out of there. We were on a highway yep we certainly were and our little hoof prints were all over it. Oh my God what had we done? We just took off fast. We never knew what we had done. I have to say years later when I returned to our crime scene I saw that highway and yes our little hoof prints were there. Those were the days what fun we had.

Then there was the time when I was stage manager the first thing I did was to drop the asbestos curtain on most of the cast and almost killed them. You name it and we did it. We were a very close knit group we enjoyed each other tremendously. One day I was helping by painting the set for a show. We did not dress up for school because we were always doing something like building sets etc and that particular day I was barefooted with cut off jeans and a shirt splattered with paint.

I was running down the stairs holding a paintbrush. I ran with my head down, not the thing to do. I ran into white shoes, slacks, shirt and blue jacket I was looking right into the beautiful eyes of a famous actor. I stuttered and said "you are pppp aren't you?" He smiled and said "yes I am and who are you?" I was beyond speaking I just stood there like a fool and he laughed and walked on out the door after winking at me. My My My …….I went back to class somehow and they looked at me and said "you look like you saw a ghost my reply was, "no it was ppppp… everyone got up and ran like a herd of turkeys down the hall. He was gone. Now that was a highlight of my life make no mistake about it.

We had fun in the evenings when we were free. There was a piano in the main area of the dorm we gathered round and sang up a storm. At that juncture of time the group known as the Entertainers were coming into their own. The lead singer and I became good friends his name was Michael Garrison who is singing with a religious group today and doing very well. They were a nice bunch of kids.

They would come over to the dorm and practice a lot it was a fun experience. They would practice their music for recordings the next day or so and we loved it… I have one of their songs which they gave me one night before it had been released. It is a great song even today.

Those were the fun times the evenings we spent together and the many hours we practiced our lines. Some evenings we had time and could take a long walk and think about the character we were playing. Those were the peaceful times. There are two types of acting. There was method where you draw from your own life experiences. Then there is technique. Technical acting is just that. It is a technique that you fake what you are feeling by looking the part and acting the part but, there are absolutely no real feelings involved it is fake. I am in the realm of method always. To me it is the real deal.

This school was magnificent in all areas. Many wanted to be directors, set designers, actors; it was all in this one school taught by the best in the business.

One morning I was assigned to a class at Main Stage. We had all gathered and said good morning to each other. I was sitting in the middle, the third row and was ready for anything. Every class was a new experience. Few of the folks were coming in slowly, I looked up and saw a very handsome man walk into the Main Stage area and said good morning to everyone. We all sat down and started the class. This man that walked in alone was extremely handsome. He was about 5 feet 7 inches fair complexion, shock of black curly hair, brown eyes and lean build. He had a wonderful smile and beautiful white teeth. I had heard of him, and his reputation was one of a really fast stepper. No wonder with those looks he was really a stopper. He came over to me, sat down and immediately put his hand on my left thigh. My heart stopped beating completely no one of the male sex had ever done that to me let alone a complete stranger. I totally ignored what he did because I didn't know what else to do I froze completely. I was taught nice girls didn't allow that, it was immoral completely immoral and just never do this at all. Well there I was frozen totally frozen and my heart was pounding so hard I was afraid he would notice. Somehow I got through that class I am sure it was wonderful I will never know I remained frozen for one entire hour. Then it was over.

This fella that came to the stage late was the infamous Eric Lawson. We all were familiar with his reputation. He was very well known among the ladies and the men because they were very jealous of him and his reputation. Eric swore that he would die at the hands of a jealous husband's hand. He was definitely impressed with himself. Almost as taken as I was and showed nothing. Absolutely nothing.

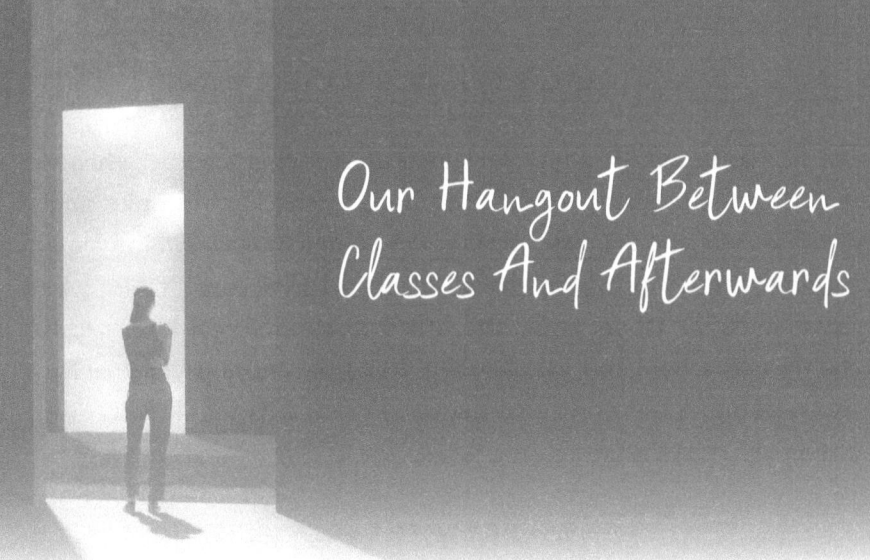

Our Hangout Between Classes And Afterwards

After class we went to lunch to a restaurant located across the alley from school by the name of Greatest Food it was a hangout for all of us and the older actors such as the old cowboy extras that were in the films of yester year. They had really good food opened early and closed late it was perfect for us. We met a lot of the old timers and visited with them. playwrights and everyone else in the theatrical business frequented this restaurant. There were a lot of film writers there too.

I left with several of the other students and made my way to the restaurant and Eric was right behind me. Little did I know this was the beginning of the greatest love of my life? Through the year we became great friends. One day he asked us if we knew anyone that could iron really well and I said of course I do am really good at it He said he would pay me to iron his good long sleeved shirts and he had quite a few of them and I had the job. It felt like Hop Sings Laundry, I went to his apartment on Fulton Street and ironed in the evenings. I ended up doing over 35 long sleeved white dress shirts. I asked him why in the world did he have that many shirts his response was well I can't iron so I keep buying the damn things. He was rarely home usually he was on a date and I didn't even see him. This went on for a long time. I only saw him at school during the daytime. I had no idea how deep my feelings for him went nor did I suspect his feelings were the same. I was very sheltered and was only interested in acting but he was in my life a lot. We ended up studying together, then we dated a few times and we had a lot in common. He was quite smart also a very talented singer. Acting, not so much; but certainly could sing like there was no tomorrow. Eric and I were inseparable. I was never so happy in my entire life. I had discovered real love. I loved the theatre, school and Eric Lawson. I had the entire package. There was nothing in the world that mattered to me I had it all everything absolutely everything.

The Season's End

We had a very busy semester. We all had huge projects to do during the semester and the more we did the more we had to do. It was very heavy a work load because we were in school all day and rehearsed every night.

When we were in a play we rehearsed after performances so it definitely was a very full schedule.

At the School, one had to be asked to return to school for the next semester you didn't just go like college, it was strictly by invitation far different from a normal college as we knew it.

Since it was a two year college I was nearing the middle and it was time to go home for the summer. I wanted to stay in Mulberry and get a job and stay in Eric's apartment that was only $75 per month which I could make easily by getting a job. That was the game plan he would go to Hawaii as he always did in summer and make money for school etc. The folks gave me a very definite NO to that proposition I was to return home for the summer. I scheduled surgery to have my tonsils taken out I was not looking forward to that at all but it had to happen they were quite bad and I could not afford to miss school at all.

We had a few days off then Eric asked me to go to San Regis with him to see his sister and mother. Of course I said yes I wanted to see something. He took what they called Slaughter Alley otherwise highway 101 along the coastline it was absolutely magnificent what scenery it was like a dream. I had often read of this particular highwas. We were going to stop and see a mutual friend that had gone to the School and quit due to lack of interest. They lived on Calico Beach and we had time so away we went it was wonderful. Stopping at Belinda's house was fantastic. I adored her parents they were gracious hosts always. We spent an entire afternoon with them and loved every minute of it. They were Billionaires her father worked for Jocelyn Rubber Company. Belinda and I were roommates for a while. I had been there before and it was nice to see the folks again. I really hated to see Belinda leave. She was a really beautiful person inside and out as were her parents.

It was getting late and we were off again headed for San Regis. It was a wonderful trip lots of grand scenery, laughs and just nice really nice every minute of it. We had a wonderful time I met Eric's mother and sister who were both extremely nice and lots of fun. He got his sense of humor honest they were a blast. We had a wonderful time. We went to the huge Zoo in San Regis;. I have always loved penguins and they had a huge case ice kingdom just for them. I stared at them for a very long time swearing they were fake and finally they moved and I was screaming with joy "they are real they are real" what a marvelous time we had" this was the greatest.

We headed back to Mulberry all too soon, I hated to leave such wonderful folks it had been paradise and a two day memory that would be with me the rest of my life. When we returned to Mulberry it was time to get the train back to the midwest. I had four days of pure heaven and now it was over.

I returned to my hometown and hated to say goodbye to Eric it was hard very hard. Two days before I left for home I completed my semester "test" which consisted of me being a stage manager for a really huge production. It was called the Magnificant Ring of the Queen it was a kid's show and had 300 light and sound cues alone so it was huge.

Actually it was the largest production we ever had to work with. My grade was riding on this monster so needless to say I was working long very long hours and was worn out.

I went home on the train because I had the time so it was a great train ride. It was on the El Cap wonderful ride it was fast very fast and covered a lot of scenic things en route. I remember they had to latch onto the train by the name of Super Chieftan because it couldn't make it over the mountains The El Cap had to pull the Chief it over the passes in Colorado. Amazing to watch absolutely amazing.

The summer was nice saw my friends, teachers and was just nice to see everyone. Then came time for me to return to the School. I had been packing a few things and Mom told me to sit down that we needed to talk. Somehow I knew I was in trouble. I could tell by her tone but for the life of me I had no idea what I had done to give her displeasure.

At that time she told me to return to the School and inform Eric we were finished there would be no more. Our "affair" was over. She kept saying, "This man is way too old for you." I was paralyzed at the thought and couldn't believe what I was hearing. She told me when I got to school to go to the front porch at the dorm, meet him face to face and tell him "last year was a huge mistake." If I did not do that Mom and Dad would remove me from the School immediately… I could no longer see him or have any contact with him at all.

I sat there in complete disbelief and felt as though my heart had been crushed to powder. I did not respond. Just looked at her in disbelief. She said "you got that?"

My response was a weak "yes, I got that" I knew better than to refute anything she said. She went on to say that the legal age for children in Colorado was 21 and I was a legal resident of Colorado and therefore they could put him in prison permanently for statuary rape, and they would do so if I did not hold up my end of the bargain.

I knew she would do it there was no question and I had to protect him I had to walk away. There was no question here, statement of fact. We weren't guilty of anything but she made me feel we were and he was at fault. This was not true it was not true at all. He was the best thing that ever happened to me in my entire lifetime.

Beginning Of The End

The next day I was on the train back to Mulberry and could hardly wait till I got there on one hand and yes had to say that to Eric… my heart was crushed and my entire world was turned upside down. To this day I have never felt that kind of pain. Guess I never will.

The train pulled into the station; I took a cab and went directly to the dorm to unpack. I did that quickly and then went to the front porch of the dorm. Eric was sitting there beaming with the biggest smile I have ever seen on an individual. I walked out straight to him and said "Hi, last year was a huge mistake, it is over" I turned and walked back into the dorm somehow. I watched him leave with a heavy heart. He could barely walk, slowly, very slowly he walked away in total confusion and disbelief. I sounded programed like a computer I am certain because I was.

I have wanted to be in the theatre my entire life from the time I was a little girl that is what I wanted to be… in the theater

School was so important to me and so was Eric I had it all for a fleeting moment in time and it was wonderful. The folks had the upper hand on me, I had to obey.

I was told to stay away from Eric at any cost and a private investigator was hired to report back to them about all my actions. I had a hard time with all this my world was being ripped apart and I didn't know why I really didn't. That is when I learned to cover my true feelings and cover them well. It was and remains a tremendous safety mechanism.

I buried myself in the theater practice, practice, practice that is all I did. I was buried totally in school work, went nowhere just buried myself as deep as possible. Eric and I were both in the same classes and that made it that much harder but I sure tried with my whole heart I remember I did my final for speech class which was taken from a Greek tragedy by Johnson Jeffers.

I did the final scene where the Godess had just killed her children and went to answer the door dripping in blood. Her Husband stood there staring at her coldly realizing what she had done. I remember part of that speech "I have met you Johnson, throat for throat, evil for evil and vengeance for vengeance. And now I go out under the cold stars of heaven, not me they scorn" and that was the end.

I finished my scene and went to the dorm. I had not been there very long and the house mother came to my room and told me someone was there to see me. I went to the front room and there stood the most famous Shakesperian actor in show business in the flesh. He extended his hand and said "my God what a voice you have in that little biddy body. I came to congratulate you on a fantastic job little lady you were absolutely fantastic I will definitely be seeing you in all the right places this is my pleasure" with that he extended his hand and I shook mine. That made my year right there on the spot. There was no doubt about that.

The year was coming to an end and we were to pick what we wanted to do as our showcase final at the School. At that juncture we were to send invitations to selective agents and various producers etc to see us in our best roles. This was to show what we had learned and the hardest of all. For my Showcase I picked a movie that showed three people in one body which I knew I could play very well. This particular play would allow me to show all three characters in the same role. It was a difficult role and my training had prepared me to do so without any doubt. This was definitely a challenging roll that would show my talent at its best and that was exciting for me to say the least. I had a lot to look forward to I really did. My goal was almost met, I could see my training coming to an end and life of hard knocks would begin but I would be acting doing what I worked all my life for and I was ready and knew it. A person knows when they are ready that is true of anything you know with every fiber of your being you know. There is no doubt absolutely none and that is exactly where I was. My sacrifices were great but I made it with flying colors.

The school had not placed me in drama or comedy I was in both categories which is rare so they said. They never found my peak which was the whole point of the school I could do whatever they threw at me and it was a pleasure I did things I never thought possible. The directors told me I was a rare find in that I could do both tremendously well. Timing was great with drama and comedy.

I had another break that was wonderful actually. One of my good friends happened to be Madelin Lakeland who was the daughter of the writer, William Lakeland that was the in the comic strip of the newspaper. He was such a sweet fella very intelligent and personality plus. He was interested in writing a standup comedy routine for me using his connections after I got out of school. That was wonderful and I was so ready. I never heard of the word fear I said "let's go!!!"

So, that was another avenue to pursue that was in my hand to say nothing of the connections I had at the Mulberry Ice House.

I confess there were times I did see Eric that no one knew about. We knew every inch of the school and met at night so no one could see us. I talked to him for hours and never told him the entire story of what Mom had told me. I never said anything about the rape thing he would have blown an artery on that one. He was so confused and no more than I. He knew how I felt and that I was pressured to do what I did. That man thought the world of me. He would leave notes in my mail box at school. One in particular was "faint heart ne'er won fair lady" I will never forget that never have and never will.

Good-Bye

Christmas was coming up and I was going home back to my hometown. I had a horrible feeling I had a one way ticket. Sometimes I could feel things deep down that come true. I knew the difference in the feelings this was real and I didn't like it. Eric and I were never seen together anywhere so there was no proof we were seeing each other. We were cordial to each other when we had to talk in class. In the play it was very obvious in rehearsals when he sang the love songs they were all aimed at me and it tore my heart out in a million pieces one at a time.

We put that play on three times twice on Saturday and one matinee on Sunday. I was to leave for home Sunday evening. We were to have a huge cast party that evening and I wanted to go for a short time to tell everyone good bye and Merry Christmas. Actually I wanted to see Eric but played the part. I arranged a ride with a good friend Ron. He did not attend the School. He was a writer and we were always good friends the whole time I was in school. Ron said he would give me a ride to the party, so I could visit with everyone and later take me to the airport. He was a super fella we maintained a good relationship the whole time I was at school. I really liked him.

The play ended, I did all the cleanup etc as stage managers do. Mission complete. Went to the dorm cleaned myself up and got ready to leave.

Ron picked me up to go to the party. We went in and visited with everyone. He gave me the high sign that it was time to go and he went to get the car. I found Eric he was in the other room sitting on the floor talking on the phone to someone. I stood in the doorway threw him a kiss and mouthed "good bye". I went to the car. The wind had come up and it started to mist. It was like a horror movie. I walked out of the apartment and heard the door slam behind me. It was Eric. He yelled at the top of his voice "Dear God don't leave me again, don't go I have rented a car I want to take you to Vegas and get married tonight don't leave me. Please don't leave me." He was standing in the middle of the street screaming at me. I got in the car sobbing and Ron said "what do I do here sweetie?" I said "drive to the airport Ron I have to do this I have to do this Dear God forgive me." That was my last memory of Eric.

A dark night, full moon wind and rain. He was yelling "don't go, don't leave me, marry me dear God marry me I love you and I know you love me." I looked back until I couldn't see him anymore. Ron felt so bad he was ready to turn around I said "no" all that time I cried the entire time to the airport which was 45 minutes to the plane. That night and memory will die when I do. That has been locked up in my heart for a very long time. Yes, I think of that night quite often I still do. I had a gut feeling I would never see him again. I was right. Well I did see him 27 years later...

The folks picked me up at the airport and headed for home. I was exhausted from the weight of leaving, the show and the emotional night. I was completely worn out. When I got home I did sleep a lot and it felt good

I enjoyed visiting with my friends and family. It was nice seeing the folks and we had a fun time we laughed a lot and it was nice.

We had a nice Christmas dinner with some old friends of ours that spent Christmas with us for many many years. They had a boy in my class at school. He died at 14 of leukemia. They spent every year with us and it was nice. It felt good to be home and be able to sleep as long as I wanted and at that I was up early just like always. Funny how that works isn't it?

Time passed quickly. It was time to return to school. I never stopped thinking about Eric and the last time I saw him. Just a few more hours and I would see him again. We had a lot to talk about. I think I pretty much decided to stay with him. I was really excited to return there was a lot ahead of me and I was ready on all the fronts. I was ready.

I had the tonsils out previously and this time it was to see friends and family time which was wonderful. It was a couple of days before leaving for

Mulberry and a friend called me from Great Plaines and said she would meet me in the City on the plane and we would have the same flight back to School which was nice and I was looking forward to it. After that call I started packing because I was to leave the next morning. I was gathering my things and pulling the clothes from the dryer and started doing the fold and stuff routine. Mom asked me who was on the phone and I told her. Dad asked me what I was doing and I said "packing" he looked at me and said "where are you going" with a surprised look on his face. I said "back to school" and laughed Mom came into the front room and said "NO you are not going anywhere." That is when the world stopped suddenly. I was in complete shock I had my invitation to return to school and that was a milestone and now Mom said I wasn't going anywhere. I collapsed completely collapsed on the floor and started crying like I would never stop and that continued for two weeks in my room nonstop. That was such a hard blow little did I know there would be more much more to come…

I never returned to the School of Fine Arts again. I was not allowed to call my friends or write to anyone ever. It was like a dream I never left never went to the School. Eric was only in my mind I gave him up in order to stay in school and in spite of it all I lost him and school, the theater training, dreams, showcase, all of it was just gone. Mom finally talked to me in a couple of weeks and she said that the school was way too hard on me I was worn out. She stated she was well aware that I did halt things with Eric and did behave myself but it was best for me to stay home and go to College here in my home town. I could not believe it no way could I accept that it was over at least I should have my things from my room. My mind raced from subject to subject… all the plans I had made for my return, the showcase, the finals, appointments with agents one on one everything hinged on the last semester which is what I was going back into. I couldn't deal with it. This was a huge shock of a lifetime. I was beyond a broken heart far beyond that but could not grasp the end of all the planning and work shot right down the drain. I had no idea it would get worse I could not imagine but it did no doubt on that.

I felt like I was living in another world this could not be happening to me I had to be having a breakdown of some sort didn't I? This couldn't be real it couldn't be. It just couldn't be happening…

I remember crying and crying and staying in my room for days. Then one day Mom walked into my bedroom and told me to get cleaned up we were going to the doctor. I looked at her and said "why, are you sick?" she said the appointment was for me. I couldn't imagine why I would be going to a doctor I was fine considering. I knew better than to cross her no way so I was obedient and got ready to go to the doctor for unknown reasons.

We walked into the doctor's office and he visited with me for quite some time and asked me to lay down on the table for a pelvic. Pelvic? What was that I asked myself, I had no idea. Mom chimed in and said it was for a girl an exam to see if the girl had been screwing around with some guy. She spit those words out this would prove whether or not I was a virgin. I was so embarrassed and humiliated I have no words for this part of my life.

I never forgot it and of course it showed I was still a virgin just like I said Eric was a good man and never at any point forced me to do anything I didn't want to do. He had complete respect for me the entire time. From that day till this I have never been treated with so much respect ever, by anyone in my life Eric was ten years older than me and that is why we got along so well he had maturity that I never encountered before it was wonderful. We were evenly matched with everything especially morals and upbringing. All of this was going through my mind as the doctor did whatever he needed to do and it did hurt by the way.

Sometimes I would write poetry or short stories at school. I loved to do that. Mom reached into her purse and showed the doctor what I had written to prove I was insane and incompetent. That's right, insane and incompetent. He read what I had written and said I was a gifted writer it was nothing more than a story and my feelings at the time I wrote it.

We left the doctor's office in silence. Not one time did Mom say she was sorry She never apologized for putting me through all that humiliating experience that I carry with me to this day. She ignored the entire incident and never mentioned it again. Mom had threatened to charge Eric with statuary rape however, with me a virgin this would be extremely hard to prove right?

When I started this story I made reference to the fact I was sheltered in the fact I was only interested in acting and the theatre. Not one time did I ever tumble to the fact Mom could not have Eric charged with rape when I was a virgin. This was kept a secret. I never told him of this, there was no contact I had no money to contact him. I held that secret for over 27 years.

After that experience Mom made arrangements for my clothes to be shipped back to me I went with two steamer trunks and two steamer trunks returned to my home. I was so excited to get my things from school. I wanted my books and things that was all I had left a few tangible items. I did get a phone call from Eric and Mom jerked the phone out of the wall and that ended rather abruptly.

It seems as though I waited forever for my possessions to be returned home. Those steamer trunks were so important because that was all I had to prove I did go to the School it was real I was not losing my mind. Then one day there they were. My whole world was divided between two trunks. Mom told me to unpack them on the breezeway so it would not clutter the house. So, that is what I did. I unloaded my trunks as I cried then she had me put all of the articles from the trunks into a garbage barrel in the back yard, saturated it with gas and lit a match. I was to stand there and watch it burn. I will never in my lifetime forget that day and that fire. It tore my heart out. I lost a lot that day. My spirit was broken and I was never the same again I lost my spirit and my dreams. I lost it all as I watched it burn in the back yard. To this writing I have no idea whether or not Dad knew what happened that fateful day.

All I seemed to think of was how everything was always taken away or it seemed that way.

When I was in college and the summer stock company was going full tilt there was one play I was not cast because Mom didn't want me to do the play for some reason I never really figured out why and didn't question just yielded to what happened. I did go to all of the performances and supported everyone and loved to be some part of it.

This particular evening I was dressed to the nines including white kid gloves which is what we wore then. I was ready to go and Mom came out with a box and told me I could wear them......this was a necklace of crystals it was a beautiful necklace and brought out the pale blue of the dress I was wearing. I was really tickled to wear them it made me feel good because I always thought a lot of my grandmother. The play went very well as usual and I went home. I got into the house and put my purse down and reached behind my neck to unhook the necklace. At that time it suddenly gave way. It broke and crystals were all over the kitchen floor.

I was broken hearted. I hadn't even got to the clasp it just broke. I guess it was old and just worn out. I picked up all of the beads and put them in an envelope and put it on the kitchen cabinet that way I could restring them in the morning. I went to bed.

The next morning I woke up screaming Mom was standing over me with a belt and really swinging it hard really hard on my back side. I remember Dad ran into my bedroom grabbed ahold of Mom and pinned her arms behind her so she could not hit me again. I have a vague memory of Dad yelling at her saying "you stop this or I will use this damn belt on you now that is enough.

What the hell is wrong with you?" I don't remember what happened after that I tried to explain what happened but she insisted someone made a grab at me and it broke. I remember saying "if that were true how did I find that many crystals for the envelope?" That is all I can remember of that incident until later that day. Mom was still on a rant big time I don't remember what set her off again but she was set... yes sir she was set off.

I had a car because we lived quite a ways from school so I drove I had lots of restrictions for it but I was a careful driver, fast driver, but careful. When I got angry I would head for the car and drive around and cool off I was not a danger when I did that, just cooled off sometimes that was the only answer truly it was. As I said she was angry all day about the necklace and something triggered her again....I was so mad it was horrible I ran for the car so did she. She, reached in the car window over me, got the keys away from me and screamed at me loudly so the world would hear her. "If you want to go anywhere you will walk you little bitch" so I did just that. I was barefooted too and it was summertime. I walked clear across town which was approximately 7 miles to where my Dad's shop was. I went to the shop he looked at me as I went to the office and sat saying nothing. I said absolutely nothing he knew he didn't have to ask. He was mad. I take after Dad when I am really angry I shut up totally and that is a really bad sign. He made a call to Mom I have no idea what he said I didn't care I just wanted to run away.

He was sick of it he was really fed up. I heard him say "this will never happen again, her feet are burnt"

I remember another time I went to the performance. Another play Mom would not let me try for was a hillbilly show so I watched rehearsal daily as I did the play before when I was not allowed to try out. I had every bit of the blocking in my head as usual almost all of the lines too funny I just remembered them. Opening night I was dressed to the nines again and headed for the tent early as usual. I arrived and Ken Conrad, the director came running toward me fast he stopped short of killing me and said "I have a rough one for you to do tonight" I looked at him and said "What Ken" his response was "I want you to do Mommy which is the lead. Connie's father died and she went home." I took a deep breath and said "You bet I can do it Ken you bet I can". So the costume fit perfect and he gave me the "sides".

I read from them. That is another way of giving lines. It is shortened and only shows the one line before the next line is yours. Kinda hard if you haven't used them before but I was at rehearsel all the time so I could handle it. That was a fantastic night. I remember that so well the audience applauded when he went on stage and said I was doing the part of Mommy and they took the place apart on the final curtain call. I went very well without a hitch it is perfect I just read the lines. It is a fantastic role and I loved it and gave it all I had. I was exhausted after the show. Everyone said they thought it was marvelous I really wanted to go home make up and all. I did so. I opened the door and mom was waiting up for me because I was late. She flipped the lights on and freaked. She said "Where in the hell have you been?" I told her and she lit into me saying well hell yes by doing that you more than likely ruined a rather stellar reputation. That's so sad you did that." And then she went to bed. And I dove into the bathtub. Well as a side note I didn't ruin my reputation it just got better by the way.

Time To Start Over

I find it quite difficult to write this but at the same time maybe it will help someone else overcome some of what happened to me. This took me a long time to get my act together. Mullberry is a small town and I knew in order to leave town I would need money which meant I relocate to a larger town and more opportunity which is what I did.

I contacted a high school friend of mine and asked if I could stay with her for a week and find a job she agreed to the arrangement and by Friday of the first week I had two jobs and had to decide which one I wanted. Things were looking up a little at least.

I was offered a job at a large insurance company and also downtown n main office for this area. I picked UnionTown to work There was more action and could learn the switchboard so I had a job in one week.

Mom helped me find an apartment one block from work which was wonderful I had no car and was on foot. I was moved in and started work on that Monday. It was a good job, benefits and I could learn a lot. I loved it. I could work lots of overtime which is fine I had nothing else to do so it worked out fine. I had some really fat checks and got paid once a week. It was wonderful. I just wanted to make money and return to school.

I had the job for a few months settled in and was doing quite well.

I was bitter about what had happened to me but never told anyone not a sole not a one.

Unfortunately I met a fella by the name of Johnny and we hit it off pretty well we talked a lot and enjoyed each other's company. His name was Johnny. We dated a bit and had mutual friends. He was OK but I wasn't' extremely impressed with him at the time. I never got over Eric and didn't want to. I spent a lot of time with this fella, because I was lonely I didn't know anyone actually just who I worked with which was fine. We dated a few times and kept spending time together so he became a habit.

Home For The Weekends

I went home for the weekends because there was nothing to do in the city by yourself so took the bus and went home. It was a Sunday afternoon and almost time for me to head back to work on the bus. I started to turn the radio on but for some reason I didn't. The weather was cold wet and drizzling rain. All at once the phone rang and it was Dad. He was at the hospital, he and Mom were in a wreck. He said he was ok. When I asked about Mom there was no response. He never answered me. I told him I was on my way… I got my brother, Chris and bundled him up good. He was two years old. I put him in the driver's seat with me and used the seat belts to hold him secured between my legs. I took off for the hospital it was one hell of a ride I was driving fast really fast. I walked in and saw Dad wrapped in a blanket Mom was in a bed in the hall. When Dad was talking to me on the phone they had not brought Mom in yet so he didn't know if she was dead or alive at that point.

The car hit a slick spot on the highway and vaulted to the middle of a strip pit on fourth street west of Pittsburg. The doctors pronounced them both medically dead. Mom had torn ever ligament in her back and legs. She had a huge knot on her head. Dad was thrown out of the car and landed squarely on his back. Approximately in the middle of the pit. When he hit the water that is when he came to. He swam to the bank took off his heavy coat and shoes he then jumped into the pit to go after Mom. He swam in freezing water (the EMT's said it was registering 13 below in the water.) to the middle of the pit to get her and she suddenly popped up right in front of him. He got a hold of her by the collar on her winter coat and swam to the bank bringing her with him.

That particular pit is straight up and down so when he swam to her and got a hold of her he got to the side of the pit and stuck her arms into the mud up to her armpits to hold her out of the water as best he could. It was wet and very slick due to the heavy rains melting snow and mud.

They were in the hospital for extended time. I called Union Town and informed them I would not be returning for an extended amount of time. I had to be with the folks at that juncture.

I remained home for quite a while taking care of things. Mom was released in a couple of weeks. She was bedfast but home I was handling the house and meals Dad was up and navigating slowly but on deck at the shop he was doing pretty well. I was really busy taking care of Mom and taking care of things, the house Dad and my brother.

I returned to the City because Mom told me to get out of the house and go home in a fit of rage. I have no idea what prompted that I just got out of there and headed home as fast as I could. End of that story.

I eventually returned to the City to find another job. Johnny of course did not know what had happened to the folks and called me when I returned to the City. We picked up where we left off eating together and visiting a lot. We again spent lots of time together.

I found another job working for Flynn's Coffee. It was horrible however it made money so that was the important thing. I stayed there for a short time. One weekend I took Johnny home with me and made arrangements for him to stay overnight with a friend of mine in Pittsburg. I told the folks I was coming home and he was coming with me. That was OK. I had never done that before but I knew other folks did that and thought I would do the same. It was innocent enough, or at least I thought so.

We went to Mulberry Friday night and planned on returning to the city on Sunday afternoon which worked for everyone. Everything was OK. Or appeared so anyway.

We got to Mulberry after work. We went to eat and when we came back to the house I couldn't get in, the door was locked. Well I thought the folks forgot and automatically locked the door. I tried the back door and it was locked too. I tried the window on the front porch and it did open. I went in through the window and when I turned around I saw Mom and Dad sitting in the front room waiting on me smoking in the dark.

They never said one word. I went to the door to open it to let Johnny in and Mom started screaming for me to "get the hell out of here and never come back." As I slammed the door I told Johnny to go to Steve's house for the night I would see him in the morning. I didn't want him to be in the middle of whatever it was we were doing here. Mom kept screaming "get the hell out of here. "You are getting exactly what you deserve which is nothing, get out of here". I turned, looked at her and said "do you really want me to go" response "yes" I buttoned my shirt, went in the bedroom and kissed my brother good by (he was only 2) I went out the front door Johnny drove over to get me and we headed back to the City I didn't see my folks again for almost two years.

Fatal Decision

We just drove straight out of town to the City and could hardly wait to get out of town. On the way back we chatted he didn't know what happened and I could not explain because it made no sense to me at all. I just said "Welcome to my world."

We talked about a lot of things on the drive back. He wanted to get married and I was in shock about the entire evening. I looked at him and said "are you for real"? And he said "as a heart attack". So that is when I decided to marry him. I could not see any other avenue at the Moment. No school, horrible job, no future at all so why not. Love never entered into it in any way shape or form. It seemed the only answer I had nothing absolutely nothing there was no future for me. I felt completely alone and could not think straight it had been horrible up till now so what the hell right? Maybe being married would work couldn't be any worse than my life right now right?

So April 3, 1962 Johnny and I got married in the middle of lent in the Catholic Church in the City It was The Church of our Lady of Fatima. We had a few friends there. We went out for breakfast after the ceremony and that was it. We had to find a place to live and a job both of which we did the following week. Surely things in my life would settle down now one would think. NO, not true.

When we went to Johnny's Mom's house she handed him the mail which happened to be his draft papers that she had for a week. She never told us so that was a blast a hard one. Then he would have gotten $150 per week that would make the rent and I would work and make the rest up ok so that was the plan. He was to leave the next morning so we had to think fast. We found him a ride to the railroad station where he was suppose to be at the appointed time I left him there and our buddy took me back home. A couple of hours passed and Johnny called me and said they would not accept him in the service because he was married they sent him home to be discharged what a shock that was.

So the plans changed again rapidly. We both needed a job however we did still have the apartment so that was good. So far this life I was leading was a nightmare one after the other and no letup in sight. What a life I had been thrown out of the house, had to quit my job to take care of folks, got married, got apartment, quit job at Flynn's, moved to West area in the City. And got another job where we had bus connections. We were both hired as a team for an establishment called the Ice Cream Freeze. It was decent and good connections via bus so it worked out well. We worked nights.

Somehow I didn't feel very good physically and blew it off to being through a lot. I was extremely tired and just felt punk.

Was I happy? NO I didn't have time to be happy or sad things were happening so very fast and adjustments had to be made swiftly. I had no idea whether or not I was happy it didn't matter things had to be done.

No word from the folks at all they completely ended our relationship so I was paddling my own canoe as best I could. I kept thinking I wanted to return. I really wanted to return to School I was so happy there. I had nothing here absolutely nothing so why not?

Johnny was ok with the idea we had to get transportation and needed money so we decided to go to and that made me happy very very happy.

We saved two weeks payroll and bought a Commander and that puppy took us to our destination. It felt so good to be back "home" I just stood there and took a huge deep breathe thinking "I am home." This was the 4th of July weekend 1963

We went to a place I was familiar with from school days. We called it the Catalina Continental Hilton Hotel. It was really old and three story with gas lights that will give you the idea how old it really was. It was one of the houses designated historical value and was not to be changed at all from the original. It had a huge kitchen and several sleeping rooms. We had one room, small bathroom and shared the kitchen.

It actually had dirt floors and yes we lived on the first floor. I remember we found pieces of an ironing board that I put one end in the window and the other end rested on the back of a chair to iron. Johnny got a job at a filling station with uniforms furnished. We could not afford sending them out to be done so I washed them in the bathtub and stomped them like one would imagine making wine from grapes. Yes, this is true. The owner of the house named Dirk did not pay the utilities so we had to go to bed really early there was nothing else to do without lights. Sometimes we were in bed at 7 in the evening light outside dark inside so the only thing left was to go to bed.

Our car seemed to realize we made our destination and therefore stopped running. It took its last breath and died. We were on foot from then on. Johnny did get a bicycle that would serve him well. It got him to and from work. We walked everywhere we went and lived in a decent place finally. It was the entire upstairs of a huge house. 124 East Fountain. It was nice, big and clean actually we were relatively happy there.

I landed a job with Western Telephone thanks to my switchboard knowledge I gained from earlier I learned like lightning.

I worked there for approximately two weeks and Johnny seemed to blow up about the entire situation he turned on me physically. He hit me very hard on the left side of my head with a lot of force I was hurt and knew it. It was painful. I had to call the office and tell them some story that I was hurt so I would not be in that day. Johnny had stormed out to work I guess I was home alone and a knock came at the door it was a representative from Western Telephone checking up on me filling out a report for the office. I told her I had opened the hall closet and a suitcase fell from the top shelf and hit my jaw She filled out the forms completely and asked if I wanted to quit the job. I was sitting there sobbing and shook my head yes. She was so nice I got two weeks pay with no problem. She was a nice lady.

I made a doctor's appointment because I just felt worse and worse yep you guessed it. I was pregnant. I always knew the first time I had sex I would be pregnant and that was true so very true.

It was a shocker for me at any rate I was scared to death and had absolutely no one to talk with just Johnny which wasn't an ideal situation at best.

The doctor was a great man. He accepted payments and as did the hospital which was Grace Memorial Hospital. I stayed on the payments making sure we could handle this somehow I thought and thought that entire day what am I going to do. What can I do? I decided I had to stick it out there was nothing else I could do.

Johnny came home at regular time and ignored the fact he hit me that hard. So did I. Sometimes it was best just to ignore things. What was the point in asking about it. In fact it did happen and we both knew it. Done and over. Iittle did I know that caused my three year battle with neuralgia. That was quite painful and nothing could deaden the intense pain.

Decision Made

Johnny sat down, looked at me, and said "you are going to have an abortion do you understand? I found a doctor we can go to and appointment is tomorrow."

I said nothing one way or the other just sat there thinking. I knew I was not going to do that so I played the game. I had to because he might want to kill me so the games begin…

The doctor Johnny set me up with gave me some pills that would cause what they called a "medical D & C" I was to take the pills for so long and report back with next appointment.

Of course the pills didn't work because I flushed them down the toilet. Yep I sure did. My mind was made up no way was I doing that. Maybe this baby would love me and I could love him or her. The two of us could have a life and hopefully a happy one. I had to get out of this mess somehow. Well of course the doctor couldn't understand why the pills didn't work and he washed his hands of us thank God.

One day on the way home from the doctor's office and a checkup I went to Eric's old apartment where we were at the School. They were tearing it down. I went up the back stairs to go in and should not have done that. It was not safe to walk around it was falling down but I had to go in I had to do that one more time. I made It no problems. I stood there for a very long time and looked around remembering how happy those days were. I was there a really long time. I realized it was getting late and I had to head for home. That was the last time I was there no one ever knew. No one.

Johnny never said anything else about an abortion from then on. I kept going to my doctor paying him and the hospital. By the time Saundra was born they were both paid for in full I was a happy camper about that.

Physically I did have some problems. It seemed I did have malnutrition and for some unknown reason my cervix was closing. The doc explained we had to have sex in order to keep it open for the birth. That is when I wanted to die, just lay down and die. I even prayed I would go to sleep and never wake up.

Well that was the worst thing in my life. This part of the story I left out. Johnny was a sex freak so I was subjected to rape almost nightly. He came in from work and said "ok let's fuck" He did a lot of damage I still pay for physically. That is enough said on that topic it was brutal very brutal and not worth talking about not going there no way. It was extremely painful the entire time.

Finally I was in labor I had false labor and the real McCoy it was pretty bad. Johnny was telling me to hurry because he was tired. I told the doctor to get him away from me and block him from the room forever. The doctor was a great man. He stopped Johnny from coming into the delivery room in no uncertain terms. That doctor was a really good doctor. He was a great man and I knew he would take good care of me and he did. I owe him a lot I really do.

My little girl was born weighing 6 lbs 5 oz she was very very tiny. She had a bit of a problem with respitory in the beginning however she was fine in the end just fine. I was released that very day late afternoon.

I asked them if I could call my mother and they allowed that knowing it was long distance and that didn't matter. I picked up the phone, dialed and she *answered*. I hadn't heard her voice in almost two years and it sounded so good. I said hi Mom you... click. The line went dead, she hung up on me. That was a heart breaker. I took a deep breath and called the shop to talk to Dad. He answered the phone and

I said Hi Dad, I have a baby girl he was delighted to hear from me. He wanted to know all about Saundra, and was I ok he wanted to know everything. He could not believe I was being released that quick but that is how they did it in California. He asked if I called Mom and I said she hung up on me. I heard the disappointment in his voice. We ended the call on a great note it was wonderful to hear him and he was concerned I was always very close to my Dad.

I was released 8 hours later and could go home which was really nice. I felt so good about that. I was to be home one always feels better at home. That first night was horrible.

Johnny of course wanted sex immediately and split my stitches wide open. I started hemorrhaging hard and was returned to the hospital by ambulance the ambulance looked like they had been killing chickens and that is true. It was horrible and I was literally scared to death. The doctor was not pleased at all and of course knew immediately what happened I was released early the next day. The next day was filled with more of the same horror, my stitches were again ripped open and I almost bled to death and arrived back to the hospital one more time. The doctor was mad he had clenched teeth. Again he asked me what I was doing and I just looked at him and did not offer any explanation. He told me he had to remove and recut part of a muscle because there was a lot of damage and he tightened me totally so it could not happen again. He talked to Johnny and threatened him with Police if this happened one more time. I could have kissed him as I said my doctor was a good man and sure did take care of me.

He even wrote the report that my two trips to the hospital were due to childbirth and therefore I would owe no more extra for the bill. He was the only kind thing that happened to me in a very long time.

I finally had time to heal. I enjoyed the baby tremendously. I walked to the doctor's office with her which was several miles and it was nice to get out and she seemed to enjoy herself. I came in from the doctors visit with her one day settled her down for a nap and the phone rang, it was Mom bolt out of the blue she was on the phone like nothing happened she was all smiles and interested in Saundra and how we were. She wanted to catch up on everything from the past two years. I was in complete shock.

Time passed and we were ok. I was doing fine with the baby and spent all my time with her she was wonderful. The day we brought Saundra home from the hospital she was on her stomach and rose up to look around and instantly rolled over on her back she was so tiny she could do that fast and very easy. She crawled early she did everything early because she was small and light weight. Ron, my old friend from the School days came to visit off and on and that was nice to see him. One day he told me Eric Lawson was looking for me because he had heard I was in the area of the School. My heart stopped. Ron asked me what to do. Should he tell Eric where I was or not? I told Ron to keep still I could not handle that. I had enough to deal with but my heart said yes yes yes. I was good I said don't tell him I can't cope.

We were always good friends. He loved to play with Saundra and she loved it when he would pick her up and play with her. It was nice to have a friend Ron had a hard life actually. He had epilepsy quite bad and therefore couldn't hold a job. He helped his Dad to do taxes he was an accountant and Ron was good help but could not be depended on. I always hated that he was a nice fella and really smart. He was also a very good writer and had a few things published. We remained friends for many years.

Johnny and I began talking about returning to the City and stopping to see my folks. Saundra was 6 months old now and things were easier with her then since she had a bit of age on her. She loved to ride and look around so we decided to go home for a visit. Johnny had purchased a car. It was a ford I think a Sun liner it drove very nice and easy car to handle. I didn't have a drivers license but that was ok he was licensed driver so I could drive with him in the car that was fine. I didn't want to drive in the where we lived the roads there are much narrower than our roads here by a long shot.

Back To The Midwest

We saved up for a while so we could afford gas to come and go to the City, packed up and headed home for a week or so. It was exciting having my folks back. I was really happy we were going home.

I couldn't believe it had been almost two years since Mom kicked me out of the house so much had happened since then it seemed like another world and another life completely. I really didn't know what her reaction was going to be. I did not tell them on the phone we were coming back for a vacation. We were going to change it. I told Johnny if she slammed the door in our face we were out of there and going to his folks in The City. My God that would have been another nightmare but… what is one more right? We drove straight through because we couldn't afford a motel. Saundra did very well in the car I was really glad for that anyway. We got to Mulberry and went to the house, pulled into the driveway and held our breath. I had Saundra in my arms and knocked on the back door. My Dad came to answer it and was absolutely tickled to death to see me. He instantly took the baby and they were immediate friends as he was with all babies. He was delighted. Mom came behind him and said hello how long are you staying? I wanted to say "until you tell us to get the hell out" but I was good said two days we had to drive back and it was a long haul. We thought about going to see his folks in Things were really bad there too. His Mom hated the air I breathed she really did actually she was a bonified mental case. I did not want to tangle with her I had enough trouble with my own folks or I should say Mom.

Honestly I can't remember much about that visit. Things were ok we were un- nerved but it was ok. We were awfully tired that was a really long drive. We chatted and they asked me about the baby etc as I said things were ok. We stayed the night and it was pleasant. The next day we packed up said our goodbyes and I took the first round of driving I had made up my mind not to return West I wanted to stay home.

I wanted to stay home in this area this is where I wanted to raise Saundra back here where we were real people and not like the folks West. I knew as she got older it would be much easier to keep track of her in a small town rather than far West. They lived hard and fast. I loved it myself but not for my daughter I wanted the same morals for her I had'. A much slower pace is what I wanted for her. As for me, I would go back no question. So, I drove away and made the wrong turn on the bypass and Johnny went crazy yelling and jumping up and down "you dumb bitch you are going the wrong way turn around." I just went faster and let him yell. I did that for a time, several miles I guess. I found a place to pull over and did so. I got out of the car with Saundra and said "ok, you want to go back here you go, carry on. I am staying right here." Down deep I wished he would have left us on the highway and gone back but no, he agreed with me and said we should stay here. He wanted to stay in the City the jobs were more plentiful there and stay with his folks till we got situated. That thought did not thrill me at all. I never even had the thought of going to my folks and letting him go home without me I wish I had thought of that but I didn't so we headed for northern part of the City we were coming home. I was happy about that really happy but not staying with his family God help me somehow. I kept remembering an incident that happened before they had her locked up. There was a wooden rocking chair in the front room. I usually sat there I could escape rather quickly if the need presented itself. She walked over to me and startled my legs while holding the yellow pages of the City Phone Book which was quite thick of course I would guess at least three inches. She looked at me wild eyed and said in a low steady voice "do you know what I do to people I don't like" and with that she literally tore that huge book in half like it was a toothpick. I never forgot the terror I felt and I never showed any fear that would have been deadly if I did and somehow I held still and blank faced. That was the only protection I had. I was shaking so bad it was horrible absolutely horrible…she was truly insane this was for real and not a movie. I was living with insanity every single day. This was far more than I could handle it was it really was.

I remember one flew over the cookoo nest was a hit at movies and everyone went wild over it. I went to see it and was extremely bored why? Because Johnny had the mother from hell a completely insane person. Now for starters the house was three bedroom, living room dining room and tiny tiny kitchen and bathroom. It also had a full basement. His Mom was not a housekeeper in any stretch of the imagination everywhere you looked there were piles of stuff all kinds of stuff. There were stacks and stacks of newspapers and clothes everywhere. In order to sit some place you had to find the chair and spend 15 minutes unloading it to have room to sit this is no exaggeration at all. They moved into that house around 1942 and had never washed the curtains that once were white lace. We must not talk of the windows, NO.I think acid would be in order to clean the windows. The Kitchen had food everywhere. One didn't know what food was coming or going, there was no way to tell. Dirty pots and pans were stacked on top of the stove two feet deep and the oven was full too. They had a full basement. I went downstairs and about died.

There were clothes all over the basement in huge piles. Here again one didn't know if they were coming or going. There were three men/boys living in this house and all three of them took showers and all peed in the shower. The smell would knock you over. In describing this I feel the bile rising in my throat as I type. There are no words to describe that horrible horrible place. I immediately considered plugging all drains, use a box of tide and turning on the hose………it was frightful absolutely frightful.

Moving along here it was also flea infested and she served us rotten ground meat and insisted we eat it. Which of course I did not do no way would that crap cross my lips it smelled rotten. When you opened the refrigerator there were stacks of bowls of old food that was growing mold and it stunk of course. I didn't know how I would live through this I really didn't. Thank God Saundra had her stroller she spent a lot of time in there. I didn't want her subjected to fleas and ticks and eating dog hair. It was the Dallas land fill I swear it was. This just about ended me it truly did. There is no excuse for any of that not one. I was living in this cesspool while Johnny was joy riding through backcountry for no reason other than a woman I am sure. He never knew I was aware of all of that. I had a job in the City and truck drivers stayed there. It was rough but I was ok they treated me ok and they spotted Johnny in the Blue Sunliner in on the way from West tothe City??? Does not compute nope sure don't.

During the three weeks Johnny was havng a wonderful time, his mother had been locked up in some type of mental facility in north of the City. I can't really remember how that came about but thanked God it did because she would have killed one of us I am certain. It is said a mental patient always turns to the one they love most and I feared for Saundra I was terrified there I was in the middle. Now I realized how Malcolm felt when he was in the middle……

I was doing some massive cleaning I brought in three of their trash bins and filled all three from the front room, dining area and kitchen. They were all filled to the brim. My father in law worked nights and slept all day which gave me a clear field. I wished we had the money to purchase a new refrigerator because it almost took a sand blaster to clean that mess. It began to look like a house now one could say it even looked nice. Saundra had room to play like other kids and loved it. It was us against the world I swear it was.

One day the phone rang it was the doctor from the facility. He told me to get Saundra and get out of there as soon as possible that "Mommy dearest" had murder in her eyes when she left them stating she was coming after me. I immediately hung up and called my friend from Union Town she picked Saundra and me up with all our trappings and took me to her home in far North. Actually it was Stone, far north of the City. I didn't call anyone I just ran I wanted no one to realize where I was they must not find us especially Johnny. There I remained with my little girl for several days. My friend was wonderful I will call her Beulah. She was kind and helped me a lot I could sleep in a clean house with real food to eat that was not poisoned. Thank God I was alive and so was my innocent little girl. I placed a call to the psychiatrist and we visited for a very long time. I told him I really thought she was skitzo beyond a shadow of a doubt and he agreed so the diagnosis was "Skitszo" with paranoid tendencies and manic depression. Man what a combo. See why I thought the CooKoo Nest was a farce? My life was more intense by a long shot.

Saundra and I remained hidden from everyone so far so good. I remained there for two weeks and it was wonderful nothing to worry about at all I was in heaven. Then, I had a Moment of reality and decided I should call Johnny and see if he was in home yet. He answered the phone so he begged me to tell him where I was and like a fool I told him. His mother was still out of the insane asylum which was greatly unnerving to say the least. Johnny came to get me and I made arrangements accordingly calling Beulah etc etc. She said it was a mistake but....I went with Johnny back to his folks house. It was not like a welcoming committee or anything but I got in and remained alive. Violet had settled down considerably by the time we were back in the house. She actually seemed pleased the trash was gone and it was all cleaned up and best of all we could see out of the windows it was amazing.

I tried to ignore everything and that was quite difficult. She was much better since she had so many of the electric shock treatments.

Possibly Leveling Off Maybe?

Johnny got a job in Town Center a pretty good one. We had enough money to move out of Hell and move into Purgatory in Avon straight north. We found a nice duplex two bedroom really nice place. They kept up the lawn we paid utilities less water. We were making it pretty much ok. We could not afford a phone and that bothered me because I felt with a child a person needed a phone. But Johnny said no there was no way.

We were there for approximately a month and he suddenly disappeared. Johnny didn't come home for three days and Saundra got really sick as babies do. It came on fast. I figured out how to keep her in the bed so she wouldn't climb out of it and she was secure and I walked several blocks to a pay phone. I called Johnny's stepdad and asked if they had seen him and the response was "'no of course not." That was no surprise. I told him I needed help that Saundra was really sick and Johnny was gone for three days. He had not been at work I tried calling there too. Jackson, Johnny's stepdad, immediately came to get us and take Saundra to the clinic.

Johnny returned home three days later and said "time got away from me". I was suppose to believe that crap. I pretended to believe it to stop a fight because he was getting meaner and meaner it was easier to agree I didn't want any more trouble at least then. We did have a nice place and were out of his folks thank God things were not the best but it was tolerable at any rate. We stayed there for quite a while. We did seem to level somewhat. We did visit his Mom very few times. Violet was really out there. We had to remember which side of the house to drive in with one side was evil and we had to remember which was which. At that time electric shock was the savior of mental patients like her. Again she had 16 sessions, or shock treatments the law was later passed that patients could only have series of 10 sessions for shock treatments. You can see how bad she really was that is obvious seeing she had 16 sessions.

It did seem to help her we could laugh sometimes like other people and did not have to worry about getting poisoned so it was better much better.

We found a small apartment in the City that was ok. Living room one bedroom and tiny tiny kitchen but it was ours and I could keep it clean. It was located on the fringes of Little Italy which was nice. Loud but nice it was ok there was a clothesline and it was so nice to hang the clothes outside so they smelled so fresh it was wonderful we survived there ok

I had been doing some research and somehow there is no way I want to get pregnant again. I had all I could possibly handle and most of the time I handled way too much. I found out there was an Clinic not far from where we lived and they would insert an IUD for $10 dollars. I decided to do that by myself while Johnny was at work. I could go late in the day and a friend next door would watch Saundra. I was not going to take very long so…….I walked to the clinic checked in and went into the room. It was like I the movies bare room bed in the middle light above the bed actually it was eerie. It was quite painful not at all as it was explained the pain was so bad I saw stars and could barely walk. I couldn't raise my left arm at all but that was ok. I paid up front and left it was a long walk home and I really didn't feel good at all and the pain was horrible. I didn't realize what I signed up for but it is over and I was surely glad. I was glad to get home. The pain finally subsided thank God. I was ok by the time Johnny got home at 12:30 that was a good thing.

I didn't want to hear it I am sure he wanted 25 kids unlike his wife.

I am sure things would blow up the minute I told him what I did but that was the right thing to do I was absolutely certain of that there was no question at all. I couldn't do that twice no way.

Things did level off for a period of time thank God. Things were easier to take and I just kept my mouth shut that was hard to do it really was. My better judgment told me to make an appointment with a doctor on the Square. I was familiar with his name and got right in to see him.

There was something wrong I kept having severe pains in my left side just like when I came from the hospital. I was relieved when I got the okay for an appointment. I only had two days to wait and was doable I was certain.

Apparently I was wrong, all hell broke loose I was hemorrhaging really fast blood was everywhere. I yelled at Johnny for help and he said "get over it you will be fine". I begged him to call the ambulance before I bled to death. No was the response I managed to put two bath towels between my legs to stop ruining everything and got to the phone to call the police for help. They came in with sirens blaring and took me to the Hospital immediately they couldn't believe what they were seeing it was bad. They got me to the Hospital in one piece. The doctors took it from there. Thank God for the police. They saved me. Or I thought so at the time. The doctor on duty put me in a room and slammed the door it was a heavy steel door and the light was like a movie one long wire with a light bulb at the end it was like a horror movie I swear.

I was afraid to move every time I did I could literally feel the blood gushing out. I was so scared it wasn't even on the charts of how scared I was. I was trembling something horrible. I lay in blood all night long. I tried to get up and sit on the side of the bed to figure out what I was going to do. It took all I had to sit up. I had bled a lot and was weak. I managed to sit up on the side of the bed and Johnny came in and knocked me back down on the bed with his fist. So I had to get up again somehow.

I will never forget that fist knocking me back down. I was thinking what am I going to do? He charged out of the room Then all at once. God sent an angel. Our dear dear friend whom I will call Murph came charging through the door. I was so glad to see him he came to me and hugged me saying "what the hell is going on here" I asked him where he parked and he showed me the car. It was close.

I was on the ground floor and this place had no screens on the windows it was an extremely old building. I begged Murph to get me out of there before I bled to death. I will go out the window to your car and you drive like hell to a real doctor. I made an appointment with a good gynecologist out at the Center. He looked at me like I was insane but he opened the window and we were on the way. We shut the door of my room after Johnny left. I have no idea where he went, I knew where I was going. Thank God Murph came in that room. He was gritting his teeth he was really mad and I knew when this was over if it did end and I was still alive we would both be beat to a pulp. Murph got me to the doctor he carried me into that office bleeding like a pig with the same towels between my legs. The doctor took me instantly got rid of the IUD that was loose and spinning around and around inside me cutting me up and that is where the blood was coming from. He made me stay there for a good while and let Murph come sit with me. I told him we were friends from years ago and he was ok.

The doctor wanted the whole story and I filled him in told him about the window thing and he could not believe it I told him they did not release me and knew nothing of where I had gone and would never know. I could never thank Murph enough for that day he was a prince a real prince. Thank you God.

Time passed somehow I was alive as was Saundra. It was touch and go but so far so good. I knew it was a matter of time and we were out of there but not yet I needed money and was saving right along and no one knew it.

I just settled into acceptance and waited for a long long time.

Settled Down In Smalltown Purchased A House

We decided to buy a house in the north end of the City called Small Town. It was nice in that location and handy to everything including schools transportation was decent since we only had one car so we decided to start looking around.

As luck would have it we found a house that was really quite decent. In the heart of Small Town a bungalow typical floorplan and it had a fenced yard. It didn't need a lot of work either and that was a plus we actually closed the deal. There was a drawback however, there always is you know. It was three blocks from Johnny's folks but I thought that could be handled. As it worked out there was no problem with that. When Saundra wanted to go see them I would walk to the corner and watch her as she walked to their house and his Mom did the same thing. It was working well. I was beginning to feel like a real person.

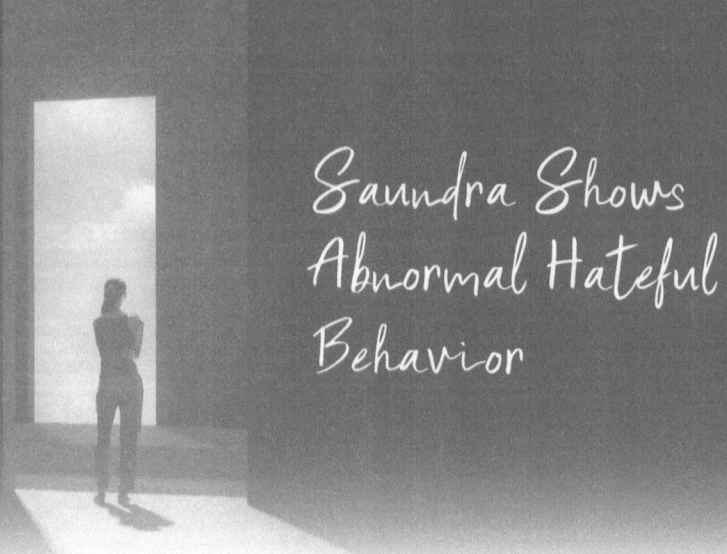

Saundra Shows Abnormal Hateful Behavior

I had noticed Saundra had taken an odd turn and I was worried about her. She seemed to have Johnny's personality which was rather sullen and she had a huge mean streak. She was a defiant little girl extremely defiant just like her Dad.

Saundra also displayed extreme meanness toward animals. One day I was in the house watching her. (She was 6 when this happened) We had a cat that came to visit a lot from down the street. I saw her pick up the cat by the tail, swing it in the air as high and as hard as she could she threw it into the garage door hard and fast then laughed. That did it. I got ahold of that little missey and spanked her rear end and announced it would not ever happen again under no circumstances that was it. She had no reaction whatsoever.

At that juncture I knew I was in trouble I didn't know what to do about it I had to think and cover all my bases.

After searching around I discovered a Neuro Center. I called and made an appointment with one of the doctors for me alone. First I had to check this out thoroughly. Then I would go from there. This would be a war with the family. Not my family, Johnny's family. They thought Saundra was fantastic no matter what she did. She was the perfect child that that was the end of the story. I on the other hand had bad feelings that there was something badly wrong and I wanted to fix it if at all possible.

I knew Johnny had a tremendous mean streak that really came out when he had been drinking there was no doubt about it. He was mean just plain mean as I knew from several hard blows I had taken from him.

I made my appointment with the doctor and took my notes prepared for anything at that point.

We did have a nice visit and he did some heavy duty "digging" to see what he could find out. I leveled with him on all fronts.

I described Johnny, his folks, my folks Johnny and his brutal temperament. I told him about me also I made up my mind in order to help Saundra I had to be completely honest no matter what I had to do she was the important one and not my job to lie and make us look like Mr and Mrs Happiness or Sunshine and Rainbows. This made sense to me. I read all of my notes and left them with the doctor. I made another appointment including Johnny. We were not bringing Saundra into this until it was necessary. I was giving the doctor an even chance with all this as even as I could at any rate. Next time it would be more intense and would keep going till something was going to change.

Johnny was displeased big time with all of this. He couldn't understand why I would do all this and ruin our wonderfully happy family.

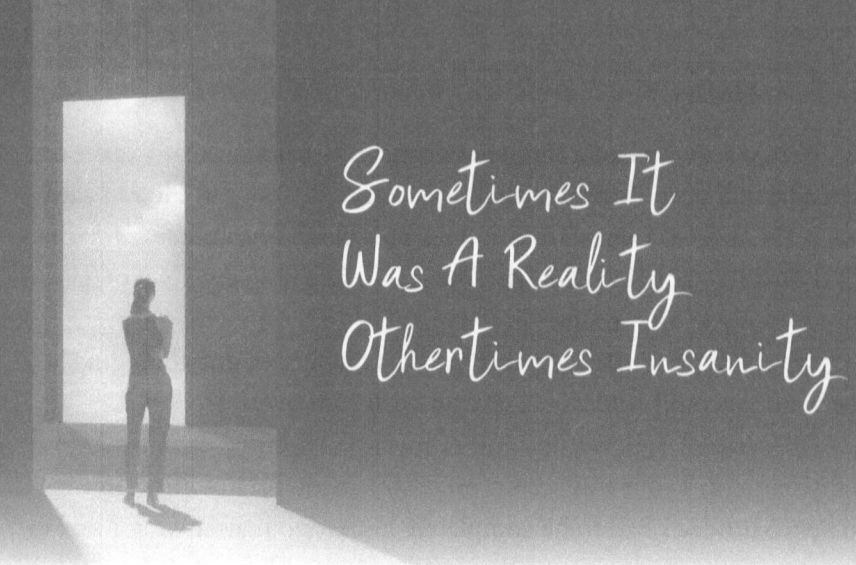

Sometimes It Was A Reality Othertimes Insanity

In the first place apparently I missed the happy part of this marriage and made the mistake verbalizing that statement. I was controlled in every single item. I did not realize any of this until I was writing notes for the doctor to help Saundra.

It was amazing how I was living or rather surviving all this. One weekend the folks came to visit and I fixed lunch for us. It was a nice day inside and out. Mom was helping me in the kitchen she was drying the dishes. She opened a drawer looking for a tea towel and said "my God what is this?" I said "What?" She said, "in this drawer? It is a little saucer of food" I instantly did the she-he-h- thing and closed the drawer. I told her "that is a food for me later. If I don't hide food I never have any to eat" At that juncture her mouth fell open in awe. I guess that did sound bad but it was true.

Even at Johnny's house his Mom would make a huge platter of port chops. There were 6 of us at the table and enough food for only 5 people there was never enough food.

At my house there was not enough food ever no matter how much I made. Johnny was super thin and ate a huge amount, always there were never leftovers so I hid food for later. I took it to the bathroom with me to eat it when I took a bath. I locked the door to have peace. Mom looked at me in absolute ahhh and so it was.

Our entertainment was going to the drive inn. In order to do that

I had to fry chicken, make potato salad and cookies to snack and also popcorn. Johnny could not go to the movie without all this to eat it took most of the day to get ready for a movie and yes there were three and we stayed all night because we paid for it. I felt like I was in the mess hall for the service the way I cooked for that man it was horrible absolutely horrible I remember the last time we went to the drive inn there were three movies like always. Saundra was in the back seat stretched out to go to sleep the third movie started.

The name of it was Blood Writer. The screen was bloody and showed a little girl that had killed her parents with a butcher knife and was using the blood to write on the mirror in the bedroom. I remembered I shuddered I always had a fear of Saundra killing me just like that opening scene just exactly like that. I never told anyone about that no one that movie scared me to death. I cant imagine I had those thoughts and fear in my heart but there it was, all the time.

I often wondered what did that say about me? That was my daughter which one of us was insane really was it me? That is a secret that no one on the face of this earth knew…no one, not one single person.

Home Became City

I walked with Saundra to school every morning before I went to work. It was nice to do that I enjoyed it I waited till she went inside then returned home.

I would catch the bus and go on to work. The phone rang and she had not showed up for school. She disappeared so I left work immediately and the chase was on. It seems the police caught her. She had gone through the entire neighborhood and dug all the dogs out of the yards that were fenced. What a nightmare it was. My days were like that every one had something like that either the school was calling or the Police everyday I had a nervous breakdown. Other little girls didn't do that other people didn't have any type of problems like I did. I never attempted to leave Saundra without me watching her every second of every day. That was a have to no matter what. She was not trust worthy at all and would throw rocks at innocent puppies and the stories went on and on and on.

I surely had a lot of ammo to give the doctors about her life at home and who else do you know that was barred from kindergarten? Or was held at the police station till Mom picked her up. I was losing ground and I knew it I was really in trouble and had no thought of what to do not a one. I just prayed that was all I could do in the few minutes I called my own when I took a bath.

I suddenly realized I no longer had any friends. I was not allowed to talk on the phone, I was not allowed to drive. Johnny drove several blocks to work while I waited for the bus to take me downtown in the City proper. Big difference there especially in rain and snow and walking three blocks to the bus.

I was completely isolated from everyone I cared about. I walked on egg shells afraid to make any undue waves I did not want to fight I didn't have it in me no way. I didn't want to fight in front of Saundra no I would not do that it was wrong so I just agreed with things and let it go.

The day came for the appointment at Franklin Neurological so we loaded up with notes (mine) and there we went. I was very nervous and Johnny was sulking. A normal day in the life and times of…

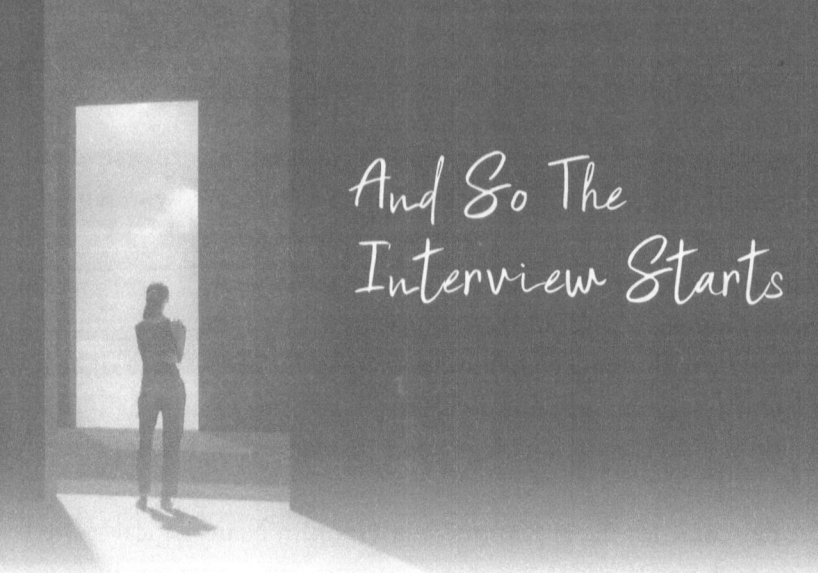

And So The Interview Starts

The doctor was extremely nice and very intelligent. He had gone through all of the notes I had given to him and also went through their entire interview step by step.

The doctor informed me he had visited with a couple of the other doctors on staff and they were certain the problem with Saundra was she was in the middle of two people with extremely different personalities. Her Dad was submissive however defiant at the same time and was entirely too physical with me. He was overpowering. On the other hand my personality was extremely strong yet was beaten way way down. He asked us about a divorce and I told him we were close to it and more than likely would go ahead with it due to incompatibility issues that even he had spotted. I went on to say I wanted the best for Saundra one way or the other.

These sessions went on for over a month. We were extremely dissected in small pieces the good, the bad and the ugly.

We had hard decisions to make or so he thought. My decision was made years ago I would divorce Johnny no matter what it took but never voiced that to any one not even at work I just kept my mouth shut and keep going to all the sessions and hoped I could straighten things out for Saundra. She seemed to be fine with all this. She was too young to really understand and that was a good thing. At least that was in my favor God knows I needed something.

Then came the day Saundra would be questioned by all the doctors on our team. She was okay with that they got to know her a bit before hand and made friends with her.

That was so sad to me. She was only 6 years old. Just a little girl and knew nothing of what was happening to us and her she had no idea and I thanked God for that.

We were to have one more session, all three of us one more time. We went home and I decided I had a week to get this divorce going so I was going to do it. We had supper that night and I gave Saundra her bath and put her in bed then I told Johnny I wanted to talk with him. He was extremely sullen that night and hard to deal with but it was just one more night to get through somehow.

The D Word

I told Johnny I wanted a divorce and was going to get the ball rolling asap. He just clenched his teeth and fists as I talked. I described how I felt which was void of all feeling and felt like a prisoner which I was. I wanted to be free. He asked what we would do with Saundra and I said I had her and a babysitter we would be fine. I did not tell him we were moving from North Town I let that lie. I said enough for one night. He was extremely quiet and I knew the storm would hit I just didn't know when. I ignored him, got ready for bed and that was the end of it. I laid there in silence waiting to be jumped at any given minute.

I spent the entire night pretending to be asleep. Morning finally came. Johnny went to work, I got Saundra ready for school after her breakfast. Then I got myself ready for work and walked Saundra to school. It was a normal day except the air was really heavy. My instincts said it was going to explode at any given Moment of time.

I decided to call the folks from work later in the day. I had to think there was a lot to do and no going back now no way. I talked to Mom briefly and asked her if they could come up to the City over the weekend. I would get them a room at the motel in Small Town, they could come in on Saturday afternoon and leave Sunday afternoon. She said they could do that all she knew was I wanted to visit with them about some things. When I got home that evening after work I made coffee, fed

Saundra and we sat down to talk. Saundra was in her room playing school so everything was calm at the moment at least. I told Johnny I wanted a divorce. He asked "why" I told him I was not happy and had not been happy for many many years and had enough I wanted out.

He said he was not going to do that he would stop the divorce. I held tight and said there is no way to stop me. I told him to get an attorney and do it quick because the folks were coming the next day and I was telling them what I was going to do.

We would sell the house split the difference and that would be the end of it then and there. Johnny was mad he was so mad all tensed up and ready to fight with clenched fists. I ignored that he was angry and drank my coffee calmly, very calmly. He got up and left to go to his folk's house saying he would be back in the morning and that was the end of it. For the Moment anyway I knew there would be more. So much more.

I sat in silence thinking about everything what would I do, when, how, where to live what about the house it was frightening very frightening. I got ready for bed and did a movie star decision......I will do it tomorrow. I went to bed.

Johnny came home around 8 in the morning. He wanted to talk and I let him as much as he wanted to. I told him I would file as soon as possible and would see an attorney Monday morning and go from there. He was in a shocked state very strange behavior but at least there was no fighting not yet at any rate I knew it would come and it would be huge when it hit.

I called the motel around noon and the folks were in. I told Johnny I was going to the motel to see them and tell them the news. I had no idea what they would say probably kick me out of the motel or something I had no idea. I got to their motel and opened the door. I sat on the bed and started talking. I told them I was getting a divorce and filing on Monday morning and get it over with at soon as possible. I was braced to hear "well we told you so, you got what you deserved but now you have little girl to take care of" and that is about all that was said much to my surprise. Thank God. They said nothing. Dad looked at me for a long time, turned and said to Mom "Well I think our little girl has grown up" that was it. I felt relieved and thought it was going to be better now. It should be anyway that is what I was thinking. I knew nothing. I was about to plow through hell literally digging and clawing my way through life with no shovel. But that was the way it was.

That all happened on Saturday and my appointment with the attorney was the following Monday. I could hardly wait It was going to be a busy week filing for divorce and talking with the doctors at Neurological Center also. Really busy week yes it was…

I felt good because I finally made the decision and felt it was the right decision. We would be ok I had a good job and benefits both would just be better with time. I would need to move from the house and that would be a nightmare to do alone but "it can be done" I kept telling myself. One step at a time. Dad asked if I had any money in the savings and I told him I certainly did $1,000. He smiled and said "Monday morning get that money out of there immediately" I couldn't understand why because half was Johnny's, Dad looked at me like I was insane he repeated "get that money out of there, you will need it for things".

I remember I left the motel room and went back to the house where Johnny waited with Saundra. He wanted to know all about it and I said "nothing to know, I told them we were getting a divorce" the rest of that day was pretty silent I told him to go stay with his folks I thought that would be best he agreed and walked out of the house not to return until Sunday that was wonderful. My mind was reeling from item to item what to do, how to handle all this, how to get to the bank with no car because he drove to work Mom called and said she would pick Saundra up and take her for the week to give me time to consolidate thoughts and we would talk later. I packed her up and the folks came and got her and took her with them for a few days. That was a miracle actually because he came thundering back into the house like an insane person throwing things around and yelling at me at the top of his lungs. I tried desperately to stay out of his way.

It was getting late and I wanted to get some sleep so I could function the next day.

I took a bath and went to bed. I just took one deep breath and he jumped on me held me down and raped me long and hard. I felt him rip me open hard, and shove me into the wall unmercifully. It always hurt me but this was unbearable it really was. I thought I would lose my mind and felt like we were there for hours and hours. Somehow I got my arm under his chest and with every ounce I had in my body threw him off of me into the wall directly across the room. He was mad really mad he wasn't finished with me and announced loudly he was not done… I told him he was done forever more he would never rape me again ever in this lifetime or the next I would die first. We continued this fight all night. I remember he laughed so loud he said "you can't prove a damn thing. An open hand hit leaves no mark but you will have a hell of a time walking or moving for a long time." He was right. The next day I was barely moving with great effort. I left early to get to work. There was an attorney at the end of the hall and that is where I was going as soon as I could get there.

I remember I went to work and told my boss I would be late but would be in and he understood. I went back down the hall waited for the attorney to open and went into his office and filed for divorce then on the spot. No thinking no nothing "lets get this done before he kills me." I knew he was capable of it and that was no joke. I went to work late but I went. Somehow I got through the day and secured a ride to the bank to withdraw the money from savings as Dad told me to do. I put it in my bank on the first floor of the building where my office was. I went home that night around 6. My attorney told me Johnny would be removed from the house in a couple of days and I was pinned there two more days two long really long days with a wild man that wanted to kill me but there I was. I started this and would finish it one way or the other.

I was seriously thinking he would kill me that was a very real probability and I knew it. My folks did not know what he was capable of I had never at any time ever told them anything of his temper.

He never showed his temper to them I am the only one that knew what he was like. I remembered one day we were in a drug store in town and he got angry at me and yelled at me really loud everyone in the store heard him calling me every name in the book. I just turned and walked out to his house and got Saundra and went home. It was horrible absolutely horrible. I hated the way I was living this had to stop and I stopped it by filing for divorce but it wasn't over yet God help me it wasn't over yet. I was so tired of living like poor white trash. I had not been raised that way and could not and would not accept that way of life. I was not going to let my little girl live that way never absolutely never.

The Temporary Moving Day

The day he was served papers at work is the day he was to leave the house legally. The attorney called me and told me he was going to be served that day for me to go home and call the police. I left work, got the bus home, called the police in North Town and told them he was being served and was to move out of the house. He was known for his temper at the police dept. that was the first time I was aware of his temper had been shown to others and the police were familiar with him. Two officers came to the house and he left under gun point. He took clothes to get buy for a while and out of the house. The divorce would not take long due to the circumstances the attorney saw to that. The police waited for him to leave and was told not to return or he would be jailed he went quietly which amazed me actually. They waited for him to be gone and told me to let them know if he returned to just call 911 they would be looking for the call. They were nice fellas they were good to me.

As soon as I could I checked all of the doors and windows the house was secured I left the outside lights on front and back and that night finally ended. I was totally spent and a nervous wreck. I managed to call Mom and check on Saundra but I knew she was fine thank God. They were worried but I was ok. Johnny stayed away from me. It was not over no way it was only a dull roar nothing more.

On The Lamb For 6 Weeks

Dad changed the tumblers in the car. He changed them all, ignition, doors. and trunk. I had three keys for the locks on my car. Johnny wanted that car no matter what. I went to the fellas at the office, and my bosses. They all helped me keep my sanity they knew what I was up against and watched out for me. They were fine with me very kind knowing what was happening. Good people they saved my life literally.

I knew Johnny was after me literally word was on the street that he had purchased a gun and he was looking for me. I paid attention all the way around when I walked anywhere. I had a fear of him shooting me in the back of the head for a very long time. I never stayed in the same place at night I kept moving every night for a long time.

I decided I would go to my folks at night till things settled down. That is what I did. I drove 135 miles every night after work and 135 miles ever morning back to the City to work. This was a killer schedule but it was safe and I could spend a little time with Saundra and that made it all worthwhile. I did get to see her a little bit at night and mornings. This went on for six weeks. Every day felt like an out of body experience. I was never late for work not one single time. The six weeks ended and finally I was to visit the doctors again at the Franklinl Center. This was to be the last visit. I was to go alone which was best under the circumstances.

I was early as usual and scared to death. I was visibly shaken by everything but time marches on and there are things one has to hit head on so here I was. God help me get past this was all I could keep saying in my mind.

I waited patiently remembering all that had happened in the not so distant past. Funny how your mind goes back and you remember all of little things that led to being here for help. My mind was gong fast forward remembering the incident when Saundra literally swung the cat in the garage door and knocked him senseless. I also remembered an incident where I was sick and came home early. Saundra was with the baby sitter down the street I called and said send her home I was sick but could take care of things. I watched for her and she came directly home as told to do. I fixed her a sandwich for supper, she chatted about her day, I cleaned the kitchen, went upstairs to bed. I put a chair in the bedroom so she could stay in the bedroom with me. I came up with some kind of a game we could play. I was really sick so stayed in bed and put her in the chair across the room. We played a game and she stood up and clapped and laughed a belly laugh. She jumped up and down while she clapped and said directly to me "I am so glad you are sick Mommy and I hope you will die" I will never forget those words never in this lifetime. Seven years old and she meant it every word. She hated me always did and it was apparent. I had a deep seated fear of her that possibly she would kill me in my sleep with a butcher knife. That is a horrible thought to have about your own daughter but that was the hard core truth of the matter. I loved her dearly and was afraid of her really afraid.

I took a huge breath as the door opened. This was it. My heart stopped as the doctors filed into the conference room.

I was seated at the table. It was quite long and by count there were 12 doctors filing in one by one to confer with me. Dr Marone seemed to be their leader so to speak. They had all examined Saundra, Johnny and me. They conferred with each other separately and together, then came up with causes and solutions this was the day. I felt like I was awaiting my execution. In a way that was exactly what it was.

Dr Marone announced they had all met with Johnny, Saundra and myself. From that they felt they could made a decent recommendation for further help for Saundra.

It was stated Saundra had hatred for her mother, I was extremely strong much stronger than anyone in the family on either side and their family of three. Saundra acted out her feelings because she didn't know how to handle it. All things considered they told me after reading all of the testing and charts It would be best if Johnny and I divorced.

Dr Marone asked if we had thought of that and I said we had and I had already filed in hopes this would save some sanity for all three of us. I admitted I had no idea how to become weaker that someone had to hold the family together and I had been elected since I was the only one that was interested in doing so. No one else was concerned with the credit report, payments on time or filing the income taxes these things had to be done and I did them. I had to tell everyone what to wear to put dirty clothes in the laundry basket and anything else that had to be done it was always up to me. I could not change my being I had tried but it did not work.

Dr Marone said it wouldn't work because it was against my nature. He said they had come up with two solutions that were viable

>**Divorce.** Keep Saundra and rigid supervised visits until she was of age.
>
>**Next.** Give all custody to Johnny and let him raise Saundra. Actually it would be his mother raising her and the rest of the family.
>
>**Results**: If I kept Saundra which legally I certainly could, it would damage her permanently. I would destroy her because I was so much stronger than her. The end result would be she would give up and be damaged the rest of her life. They also agreed that she literally hated me and everything about me. Unfortunately she hated everything I stood for.

This was the choice I was given. I set there in shock and shook my head I could not comprehend what they were telling me not even close.

I looked around the room in utter disbelief and said "I am sorry I do not understand what you are telling me."

Dr Marone came over to me and said "It is quite evident you love that little girl with everything you have. Now what we are saying quite simply is "Do you love her enough to give her up?" I said absolutely nothing. It was hard for me to breathe, very hard. I picked up my purse, looked around the room and thanked them for all of their time and honesty. I walked to the door and stood there and looked at it for a long time. I turned around and said "good bye, I will call you tomorrow."

I couldn't drive home that night, there was no way. I called one of my girlfriends and asked if I could stay the night with her and of course I could. She had a date and I was glad.

I needed to think. I took a shower hope against hope somehow I would self destruct but nothing happened. I didn't know what the problem was....the answer was obvious. I had no right to keep her and ruin her for the rest of her life. That was not the thing to do. She had every right to be happy. I was having trouble with the thought my daughter hated me. That was a hard one. I could do nothing about that. You can't put love where it isn't. That was a very hard blow to accept. I was numb totally numb. I also knew it must be an absolutely clean break. No Christmas cards, presents, birthdays etc. totally gone. By doing that there was absolutely no way their family could throw me up to her about anything which of course they definitely would do beyond a shadow of a doubt. I would remove the lever completely and that would protect her from all accusations. It would be rough but she was worth it.

That was my decision. In the due process I discovered after a lot of research the only state that would protect me is Louisiana. So I decided to pack and started doing so. Then sanity took over and I realized if I did that I would be running for the rest of my life, I decided to unpack. I had a good job making good money and was well established in the

City so I was going to stay in spite of everything what was one more fight right?

So this had ended. No more wondering what the results would be there would be no more guessing and what if. It was. So be it, move on.

The Next Huge Wave, The Divorce Itself

The actual divorce was scheduled to be in Liberty Missouri. Mom said she would come Saundra was with Dad. No problem there. I never quite figured out why but we were taken into the Judge's chambers before the actual divorce. He wanted to visit with all of us before actual court.

As it happened that was a very good thing because there is no way I could ever explain what happened in that room. No one would have ever believed me there was no possible way.

The judge stated Johnny had visitation every other week as long as he kept the child support payments current in the amount of $35.00 per week and on time, always. He was to leave us both alone without undue harm. Johnny wanted to add a couple of things and the Judge allowed him to speak.

Johnny told the Judge he wanted weekends, overnights with his meals included.

That is when it got insane. I jumped out of the chair and lunged across the table and put my hands around Johnny's throat and screamed as loud as I could "you dumb son of a bitch this is why I want out from under you. I want the bed privileges removed totally and no more food. I am done" No more bed rights no matter what.

The Judge thought I was going to kill Johnny and I wanted to. My God I served my time I was so done there were two officers that pulled me off of him in chambers. My mother could not believe what she heard and saw. If she had not been there she would not have believed it at all. Welcome to my world of insanity.

When things settled down I was to get the house and car due to the fact I would have the child and needed transportation and place to live.

When it was over I was walking down the front steps of the courthouse. Johnny walked over to me crying wanting to start over and I looked at him and spit right into his face and screamed "YOU FUCK OFF." Those were my final words to him from that day till this.

Now The Games Begin

We were married for eight years and during that time I was not allowed to drive the car anywhere for any reason. I did not know my way around Kansas City for that reason.

After the court hearing I was beat as was my Mom. She told me we needed to find a place to live and I had no idea how to do that. She said "you have been driving since you were 14 and there is a car in the driveway. Put your ass in the car and lets go."

It was raining and I was terrified but I could still drive yes, I could and we did including the interstates it was amazing absolutely amazing. We drove around for awhile so I could get use to it again.

The next day Mom had to tell me to get up, to go to work etc. I absolutely had no capability of my own.

I could not think for myself at all. It was like I forgot everything or ha*d a* stroke. It was sad really sad she had to tell me everything to do all week. Mom planned to stay till the weekend and we would go to the folks. It was nice to go back home it was safe and I was relieved to be there. I was so happy to see Saundra with no worries of being killed. I knew Johnny was out of his element and I was completely safe.

The game plan for me was to return to the city and move from the house. Dad put his foot down on that. He said it would be better if I stayed out of the line of fire and he and Mom would go to the house and get a few things that I wanted. At that Moment is when I leveled with the folks on Johnny's temper and how bad it was really. I told Dad never to turn his back on Johnny that he would take Dad from behind. If he had been drinking he was one mean s. o. b. bar none

Dad took a little ball bat with him and said no problem. When they left it felt like the end of an era, total relief just Saundra and me. I had a lot to do but for a few wonderful minutes I was fine with my little girl that I loved more than anything in this world just the two of us it was heaven truly heaven.

The folks were ok they made it without incident. Johnny was there but was broken hearted and whimpering like a child. The folks got all of the pictures which I thought were important for Saundra to have some day.

I had a feeling it would be a nightmare for a while and I was right.

When I went North for anything at all I would find a hangman's noose on my front door of the apartment in Independence. There were threats, notes etc.

The divorce decree stated we would have Saundra every other holiday. The first thing that happened was Johnny stated he wanted her on Christmas which was a nightmare too. His family did not believe in Christmas and I did. I wanted her to always have a nice Christmas with a tree and everything little girls should have. He called me at work and told me he was picking her up for Christmas knowing it crushed me so of course I agreed what else I could do for God's sake. So we made those plans on the phone.

What Johnny did not know was I had an appointment with a crackerjack attorney in far North Stone that evening about Saundra. Steven Cranshaw. He was great. I called Steve and told him what I had and he said he would wait for me that night. It was a pretty good drive from downtown to North Stone but I made it pretty close to 6 that evening.

I told Steve what I was up against he shook his head and said he knew because Johnny contacted him for divorce and Steve turned him down. Steve went on to say Johnny was a bum and noted for it all over the city especially in the community where he lived. He also said he grew up right down the street from Johnny when he was just a kid and he was mean then. I told Steve I also wanted my maiden name back along with the full custody of Saundra to Johnny. He said January 2 I would be me again and Johnny would have full custody Steve explained that in time the books would show that I abandoned Saundra that was a legal thing. He wanted me to know that. I understood completely. I also told Steve I did not want Johnny to know. When he picked her up for Christmas he would have all of her possessions at the time and I would say I was out of town for two weeks and it was over. Steve said he would call Johnny and bring him to the office and give him custody. I said what if he said no? Steve laughed and said he won't he will sign the paper and it is done. Quick and clean.

Now you go live your life and if he ever bothers you again in any way at all you call me and let me know. I have enough on him to put him in the big house for many years and I will do it. He knows I will. You are free completely free of him from now on. I gave Stephen a huge hug and said Amen! This chapter is over.

Finding A New Home

I found a nice place to live in Independence. I was thirty minutes from work but it was very nice and secure. Two bedrooms huge kitchen and front room. The bedrooms were upstairs along with the bathroom. It was a very nice place lots of room and really clean. I knew it would-be cheap to maintain as far as utilities. I was elated with it.

Mom and I were sorting some boxes. I found a square of onion skin paper and opened it. I could not believe what I saw. It was from some small town in Kansas where Johnny had been picked up on suspicion of murder. I knew he was cold blooded and I was correct obviously. My mouth dropped open who knew? God helps fools you know.

I found a baby sitter right down block walking distance and that was nice too.

One of my friends at work wanted to car pool and we traded weeks and it worked well for all concerned. She was divorced with two kids about Saundra's age and we had lots in common. She was in a house in fifteen minutes from me so we had it made. We got the kids together and they had a blast everyone got along and it was nice to have someone with something in common with me. It was lonely and she filled the gap we both had it was wonderful. We enjoyed the relationship tremendously.

Christmas wasn't far away just about three weeks so that is when the custody thing would be handled. I enjoyed Saundra while I had her. She didn't suspect anything no way she could. She was 6 turning

7 in January, January 24 to be exact. Johnny did see her every other weekend. The weather took a cool dip. She had winter clothes and a nice coat that was warm gloves and a hat to match. She would come in from her visit with Dad and came in out of the cold with no long pants, undershirt, hat or coat on. Sometimes she came in barefooted I could not believe it. She would throw down her clothes and walk on them coat included. She had no respect for her clothes whereas before she did. She realized it was her job to take care of her clothes. I knew what I was in for she would have no training at all. When she stayed with her grandparents there were no hours for bed time. She would lay in the middle of the floor and go to sleep till morning in same clothes. This was foreign to me but that is what made her happy. This is what I could not handle at all that and many other things. She never seemed to care and I could not teach her to care, or to love animals and respect them. That was a total lost cause. I tried so hard to show her respect, love, etc but it fell on deaf ears.

I remember the day Johnny was coming to pick her up for Christmas. I helped him load her things in the car. He said wow she sure has a lot, I said yeah she sure does. You can bring her back on January 3 I will be gone for two weeks. He went off and said "I can't do that I work" I said "well I am off and not going to be here so you will have to figure something out. I had this planned for a long time"

I walked back to the apartment to get Saundra and put her coat on she said nothing just goodbye Mom and that was it. I told her to be good girl and that was the end of my short lived motherhood

My little girl was gone and she took with her all my hopes for a happy childhood for her and every dream I ever had of a happy family. She was happy but not with me she hated me and I had to accept that. It took me a long time to come into the reality of the situation. She never looked back that day not once.

I went inside for a few minutes and got the Christmas presents for the folks and my brother loaded the car and was on the road. I got a phone call from the attorney on Christmas eve telling me I had my maiden name back and Johnny had signed all papers I was free. I didn't know how I felt I was pretty numb and remained that way for a very long time. The good times were not in the picture. I was beaten down very unsure what I was doing and why and really didn't know if I could make it alone. I had no one really this was a lonely road and I didn't like it. What was amazing about it was no one ever asked me how I was, no one.

A few years later Mom told me she didn't think I could make it through all of this and Dad disagreed with her he said I would walk through it and be fine in the end. He was right but we never spoke of the incident again. I never mentioned it because no one could understand because they didn't know the entire story. I had one good friend Pat, she knew the entire story and she never flinched not one time because she knew it all. I needed her friendship badly and she was there, always. Most thought I just didn't want her and I was a bad person for giving up my daughter. Ironically I gave her up to save her. I had no right to destroy her I gave her a fighting chance with me removed from the equation and that is the end of that story.

I had made plans with the fellas at the garage that worked for my company. They agreed to hide my car and keep it hidden until the heat was off. I had it hidden during the daytime, drove it home at night and hid again during the day. What a mess. The fellas were good to me very good. I paid them a little bit to do that for me and they took good care of me. They were a blessing as was my company, always. Maybe it is over, right?

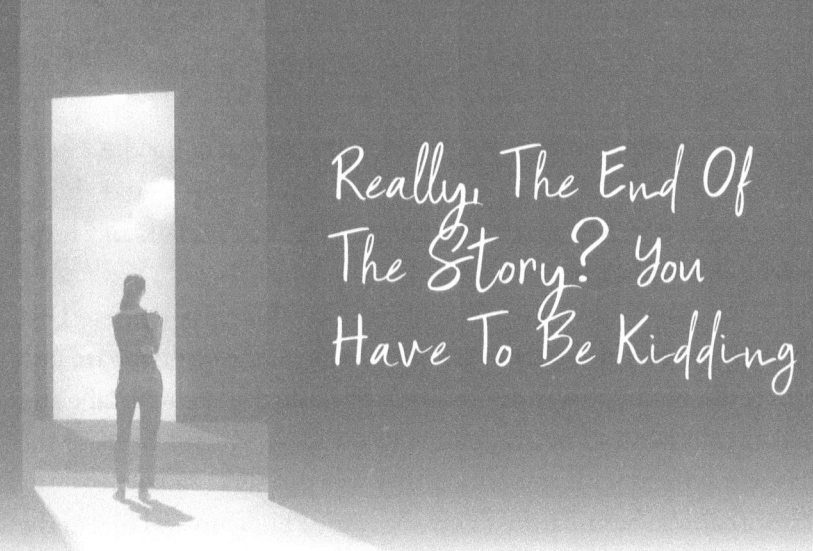

Really, The End Of The Story? You Have To Be Kidding

This story never ends in many respects it just started. I was married eight years to a tyrant and now I am single, no children, no future only a past that I choose not to think about. No more Christmas planning, no more game playing, play days, movies, popcorn, reading books…….all gone absolutely everything I cared about totally gone. Marriage? that was not one of the fantastic dreams a girl has. I missed it all. Dad sat me down and talked with me. He told me that" later on if I was interested in someone enough to possibly marry him I would have to tell him of Saundra." He went on to say "nothing should be hidden and if this fella could not accept what happened then walk on by that he was not worth the thoughts of marriage." I loved him for being so horribly honest but truly I was not interested in getting married again ever. Right now I was just trying to survive let alone any future thoughts of anything. No way. My mind was vacant I think that is a good word to describe my mind at the present it was extremely vacant. Nothing was there absolutely nothing.

What did strike me odd a bit later was Mom never asked me how I was or how I felt. She never talked about it ever. I could have used some backup then actually. My mind was gone. And I had absolutely no thought of the future. I just took one hour at a time and managed to get through them somehow. I returned to my job and straighten up my new apartment. I shut Saundra's room and didn't open the door for a year. I couldn't do that I just sealed it up I guess for the rest of my life who knows. My plan was now one day at a time and things were getting better. My apartment looked nice. Car was ok and I was ok maybe this will be ok after all.

The first thing was to gather all of the sheets and give them to Dad for the shop he would use them for rags. I was on the switchboard and answered the phone it was my mother. She asked if I could talk and I could then. Dad told her to tell me to go to the doctor because the sheets were stained with something that was not right in color.

Now that was humiliating to say the least. I hung up and dialed the doctor. I told the receptionist there was a problem and she immediately took it from there and the doctor made an appointment for me that very week. This would be put into the humiliation file of course. It was coming from all sides periodically I was still numb for everything that happened to me. I was past rage and hatred I was completely worn out with everything absolutely everything.

The day finally came for the appointment. I was blessed with a really good doctor. We could communicate with each other. He was well aware of my situation for many years and he had the entire file. This was just one more. I told him what Dad had said and he smiled and said "he was correct he would know. Normal seamen are clear which he knew. It is a good thing he told you to come in we can fix you with no problem at all". The next scene was me in a complete shambles in his office. I remember I Just sat in his office and sobbed for a very long time.

When I finished I sure felt better. He gave me a shot and said I would be fine and he gave me a prescription for antibiotic to take for five days. That was it he said it was all good now. It was amazing for some reason my mind went back to when I was in the City with Johnny. I got sick with some infection and the doctor gave me a shot and pills that we both had to take… I thought my God what was I exposed to then talk about stupid I sure was I was insane and God got me through all that and this now I am so thankful. I went back to work and finished the day. I went home that evening and watched TV it was the first normal night I had in a very long time. I checked the house several times I wanted to be certain it was all locked including windows and the basement was secure.

Peroid Of Adjustment

I began to unwind very slowly but I was doing very well. I took one day at a time until several months went by and all was good. I always watched behind me the fear of being killed never left but it was getting better. Usually I went home to see the folks on the weekends leaving on Friday night returning around noon on Sunday. It was a nice drive and I had time to unwind. We visited a lot and I found some old friends I knew and went to eat with them. They knew nothing other than I got a divorce and that was nothing just a statement of fact.

There was a new hire at work by the name of Ed he wanted a job with our company and he was sitting in the reception room with me for approximately two weeks all day every day just waiting for an interview. One day we had an opening and his dream was fulfilled they hired him. By that time he and I were good friends and remained friends for years. Ed happened to me at a perfect time. I had nothing in my life at all nor did he.

To my surprise he had been married only three months and he and his wife were in a horrible car accident. She was killed instantly so he too had a lot to overcome. We drug each other out of the messes we lived through and began to laugh again. I had never had such a wonderful friend in my life. I let him into my world with open arms and he did the same for me. For the most part we were always together. We would walk to the Waterfront by the office after work for coffee and just chatter.

It was nice it really was. Off and on he became interested in a girl and told me all about her it was fun great fun. I didn't have anyone didn't want anyone I had a wonderful friend that could not have been closer if he had been my brother.

Ed and I became responsible for decorating the office for Christmas ever year. It was elegant we didn't have anything at home so the office was very important to us we went shopping for a huge tree that looked like Sequa Forest, decorated it, the walls and I piped in Christmas music into the office. We had the best decorated office of any clients anywhere. Then, I got to thinking....I talked to all of the girls in the office and picked a date which was a Friday and had everyone bring something home made for the fellas and we had candy etc on every desk in the entire office of 50 we all kept the secret and bang we hit them with it. I fed the outside so had lots of cooking to do and called the suppliers to come by for a little something. They all came and enjoyed Christmas the entire week it was fantastic. Ed and I made a good team. We loved doing that it was truly a joint effort. It was good therapy for both of us and we had each other. We ended up decorating the office for eight years. It was eight years of laughter instead of tears it was wonderfully full to the brim of laughter.

There was a fella in the PR department that befriended me and we became very close. Yes he was quite a fella and his name was Karl. Along with his PR job he was a free lancer and made the same as full time salary. A very accomplished writer for the agency too.

He was also a pro photographer and taught me the art of taking a good photo and also printing them in the agency dark room on weekends.

He was a great teacher and I was a great student. He taught me quite a bit about writing and also taking photos that said things not just a flat picture. Sometimes we would shoot on the weekends and develop the following weekend. One time he was writing a story about the Hyber boats in Minnesota I think. There was a huge race scheduled and he was covering it. He wondered out into the reception room and asked if I would like to go on a shoot in Minnesota of course I did. He told me to pack we left the next day after work. It was a 13 hour drive one way. We left on Friday night and remained awake all weekend and was at work on the following Monday. Man that was rough. We were both shooting the races he was on one side I was on the other and away we went as fast as we could hit the trigger. It was fantastic fun not like work to me. We ate the brats they had and they were fantastic everything was. He wrote a great story about the races and the photos were grand. He promised me a fish supper of Walleyed Pike which is heaven when it comes to fish. As a kid we went to Minnesota and caught them man could that fish fight so could the Northern Pike. Karl came out to the reception desk and showed me the photos I took and man, I got some great shots and took the cover. He was the pro and I took the cover what a laugh we had for that one. He was proud of me because he did all the teaching. He offered to give me the money for the cover since it was only fair but I turned it down. I got paid with the fun and learning I had no problem with that at all. He and I were a good team also for many years. We never claimed it however it was best we didn't this would not have been good if anyone knew. Between he and Ed I was in wonderful company and had a life filled with fun, laughter and an amazing life that developed slowly and very steadily. I came into my own I was happy really happy and learning a lot at the same time.

    I had two best friends I would not trade for anything. Ed and Karl my PR fella we were a tremendous team.

    It felt good to be happy again, it had been many years that I had not laughed or had any fun at all and I was coming back it had been slow but I was becoming the person I use to be and I liked it. I had not been happy for many years and it felt so good to laugh and have fun plans. My two buddies were wonderful absolutely wonderful.

    I was amazed at the life I had carved out for myself however, I never forgot Eric Lawson not for a minute nor the fantastic School of Fine Arts for Drama. I never mentioned either of them but those two things resided in my daily thoughts no matter what.

    I went to see a rock opera that I loved at least 13 times it was amazing absolutely amazing with the original cast for some reason that show brought it all back and the love of the theatre was always with me but that was buried way down deep and remained there as did the memory of Eric Lawson.

One day bolt out of the blue Karl called me on the intercom. He asked if I wanted to go to Pasadena for three days. I was in shock and couldn't say much there were folks in the reception room. Karl told me he was scheduled to do a story and would be at the where the millionaires were for three days and wanted to take me to see my friends.

I couldn't believe it I could return and see my buddies? I could actually return to the happiest place on earth? I was speechless absolutely speechless. My answer was absolutely I will be ready in ten minutes. This was amazing absolutely amazing.

I managed to get the extra day off work without any questions. They were good about that I could usually go whenever I wanted to I had proven my loyalty to them time after time and I was fine.

I secured a ride to the airport without issue and we were on the road West. No one knew I was coming absolutely no one and thinking about it I was taking a huge chance but I didn't care I was going back to the greatest place on earth to me anyway. The flight was on the L1011 the same plane that not long before had the tail fall off. Yep that was it. That plane was huge it was a monster three across the largest plane I had ever been in huge it was wonderful. We arrived at LAX, secured our car and were on the way to Millionaire Bay where the millionaires docked the boats, of all types it was quite a sight to see. Of course I had seen photos but the real McCoy was totally breath taking it truly was.

The tricky part was checking into the motel that had not crossed my mind I was so happy to be there. Karl got one room and I got nervous he looked at me and said "settle down got you covered the company would frown on me wanting two rooms so....we have a huge room with two king beds and I am certain we can handle it." I agreed to that I had complete trust in him and he proved to be extremely trustworthy. It was fine it truly was. We went to eat at the small waterfront cafe which was directly on the beach fantastic view and he had a bouquet of gardenias delivered to our table talk about a night to remember it was that and then some. I was living a wonderful dream and it was very enjoyable. I still have the room key.

The next day we got ready and headed for my town and we were at Central Blvd and El Esconda and I said "ok this is fine just drop me off here anywhere I am in familiar territory all the way around"

He screamed and said "I am not going to pull over and drop you off in the middle of nowhere without any idea where you are or if you are ok." He had a cow right there in the car.

I told him to pull over and park so we went into the restaurant and I made a telephone call to one of my buddies who screamed and said "stay there I am on my way". I looked at Karl kissed him on the cheek and said see you tonight at 6 right here in this spot. He left me there and a wonderful day ensued.

Ron was my buddy that took me to the airport when I left school for the last time it was nice to see him again. It was wonderful absolutely wonderful. We sat down and chatted up a storm nonstop. Then I remembered another fella that use to work in the book store. He was third poet laurelthere and we went to the book store where he was waiting on a customer.

I went in behind him until she left and he turned and took a double take and literally screamed he swooped down and picked me up with his huge arms it was wonderful. He was a sweetheart. Sean was a huge man he was certainly not fat he we just big boned and a lot of him His voice was booming he was wonderful I felt so tiny in his big arms it was fantastic to see my buddy again. We all went to eat and again chatted up a storm. His boss gave him the rest of the day off due to circumstances. When we were eating I asked if anyone knew anything at all of Eric Lawson and no, they had no news at all of him other than he looked for me a very long time. I let it rest for this time.

When we had time to talk between us Karl told me we had to go back to our City earlier than anticipated it seems his story fell through the floor at the last minute due to industrial espinoge. His story folded and so…

I about died I couldn't handle that kind of news no please. "since we are here and will never return lets go to the Beach and take the tour of the Queen while it is there and we are here. One more day will not kill either of us and we will never pass this way again.' I talked him into it so we had a day and a half that was ours. We went to The City where I had gone to School and I showed him the School, and the infamous City Hall where a lot of movies were shot he took many many pictures we had a wonderful time and lots of laughs We did make it to the Queen and that was a fantastic tour and many many shots there too. It was like a mini vay and it was outstanding. I don't remember having so much fun it was like two kids out of school. We returned to the city and said nothing of the fantastic time we had that memory was ours forever and only ours. It was one of those memories you never forget and think of them as the years go by and that is what we did. As a matter of fact Karl and I kept in touch many many years. Unfortunately he passed away two years ago of a heart attack. Ed and Karl my two best I lost but I thank God I did have them I was the luckiest person alive, yes I had two best friends. I loved those guys and still miss them.

Relocation One More Time

As the years passed I became restless working at the ad agency. It was a great job but I could do so much more than answer the phone. I even carried the PR Department while I ran the switchboard which was quite a feat. I wanted to do more with a lot more responsibility but they did not want to move me from the switchboard. I was very well known and well liked hence no transfer. At one point they had Southern Bell were the switchboard to tell how many calls came through in a day and it clocked one thousand calls I averaged answering the line and connected it to the party desired in less than ten seconds which was a fantastic record for anyone. I definitely was the best and my pay reflected that.

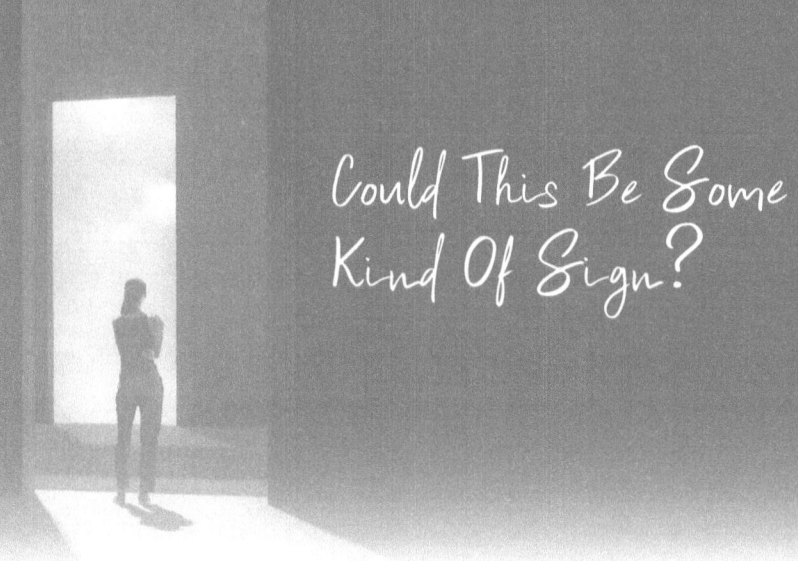

Could This Be Some Kind Of Sign?

I needed more to do seriously I really did need more to feel like I was worth something. I decided on a fluke to write a letter to the radio station in my home town and the television station called me talk about a surprise

I couldn't imagine the TV station calling but there they were at the other end of the phone. They wanted to see me ASAP. I said ok and made arrangements to visit them to interview.

I could not believe what had happened never in my wildest dream could I imagine something as remote as this happening but here it was and there I went.

I interviewed for several jobs when I was there they even gave me a shot at doing the news anchor (I was not remotely interested in that at all, no way) I was very interested in doing the TV productions and had a feeling they were leaning towards sales secretary due to my communication skills.

I had the sales secretary job before leaving the station that day. I had two weeks to move from City and relocate to my home town. I thought this was delightful.

I returned to work on Monday morning and turned in my two week notice. This was not received well. A raise was offered to sweeten the job but that did not work I wanted to go home. I did settle with them for a thirty day notice due to all that I did on the switchboard. My job had turned into sort of a trouble shooter used when and where ever I was needed far cry from just answering the phone. I learned a lot and loved all that I did for everyone. This job had become my family and it was very hard to realize I was actually going to leave. I would leave Karl and Ed two of my very best buddies in my entire life....

I wanted to go home. I sure did.

I called the TV station and asked if they would wait for me for thirty days and they agreed and said I was worth waiting for. I was delighted. Not so at the agency.

The president, vice president and all the rest of the big guns talked with me and wanted to know what would make me stay it broke my heart but I loved my home town and wanted to go back to my small town with a much relaxed atmosphere. And so the clock begin ticking.

There was a lot to consider. I went home every weekend to find a place to live and finally found a house.

I knew I had profit sharing from the office and could swing the deal and I did. I had my own house I couldn't believe it.

I began building a life again one thing at a time. The time actually flew by and the day came to say good bye to my Agency family. My wonderful people. I had to say good bye to Ed but he had helped me move and our bond was unbreakable. He had been to see the house and had a wonderful relationship with my folks they adored him as did I. Karl would come visit but not often however he certainly did use the phone a lot and for that I was so thankful. Thanks to him I made the utility room into a wonderful darkroom for printing my black and white film. It was a wonderful hobby absolutely wonderful. I would not lose his friendship so my world was getting larger not smaller and I thank God for that many times over.

I moved the month of June and proved to be ideal. Flowers were blooming, birds singing and I had a new house and job it was wonderful.

Ed came to visit over the fourth of July and it was a great visit we had a blast with each other and the folks too. It was a grand time. He and I went blackberry pickin and Mom made a wonderful pie. It was a perfect day absolutely perfect summer was beginning. I did get to take

Ed to the TV station and introduce him around and he enjoyed that a lot and I did too. It is always nice to share things with someone isn't it?

Ed came on the bus this time his car was sick and I took him to the bus around 1pm. It was a perfect ride back to the city I made it many many times myself. That was July 3. I sent him on his way home after a great visit. The folks left on vacation to Brownsville and my brother and I were left to watch the homesteads.

I didn't work the next day which was the 4th of July. I was sitting on the patio having my coffee and I looked up to the beautiful white fluffy clouds and I remember saying out loud "Ed those clouds are moving fast which is high wind I so hope you are not sailing today even though you love it. That wind is too much today Ed too much." I had a horrible feeling that was choking me and I shuddered horribly. I didn't know why. My horrible feeling of loss was heavy all day.

I woke the next day early as usual. The phone rang at 6:30 no one ever calls that early in the morning unless there is something wrong.

The phone rang. It was Karl. He said "are you up"? and I answered "of course I am always up. What's wrong Karl?".

"Ed is dead baby, your buddy is dead". I could not comprehend what he was saying my fantastic friend I shared my entire life with was dead? He was sailing, on lake Jaca in the City heading for the dock coming in and fell. The under current got him and they just found him thirty minutes ago. He had been under for 24 hours. His friend, Kennedy was there with him he asked if Ed was ok and the response was NO He threw a life preserver and Ed went down. They found his body wound in under growth the next morning early.

At that Moment my soul was ripped from my body literally. I thought of my brother he loved Ed so much and I walked down the street. He apparently had looked out the window and saw me weaving down the street. He threw open the front door and screamed "what is wrong?"

I screamed "Ed is dead" and he collapsed right there on the porch. I helped him up and together we went into the house and I repeated what I had been told.

Now I waited for arrangements that would be forth coming. We stared at each other in complete disbelief…

We sat there for a long time I guess. The phone rang, it was Mom. Her first words were "what is wrong?" I told her and she and Dad were both floored with the news. They both broke down I was still in shock. She said there was no way they could make it back for the funeral I told her I had it in control. My brother and I would go and help each other somehow. And so we did.

I finally went home and sat with a cup of coffee and stared at the wall. I was there most of the day neither one of us could function. The folks called several time to check up on us.

The word came in about the funeral when where and the time. So we made a plan to go. The friend that was with Ed on the boat was also my good friend. I felt so sorry for him it was my understanding he was on heavy drugs at that time.

He was not handling it well at all and that is understandable. I didn't handle it well at all I was deadly calm I remember that well. I was numb my entire body was numb. I needed to contact the other fella and could not function try as I might. His name is Kennedy.

Kennedy threw the inertube to Ed several folks saw all of this happen. Kennedy was functioning but not well at all.

I told my brother Chris that we would make it one day turnaround trip which was fine.

We went to the agency the day of the funeral. They did not want me driving so they made sure I was ok and so was Chris. We were ok I guess everyone wondered about me and my reaction to Kennedy the first time I saw him. We went into the back door I headed for Kennedy first.

I saw him and was glued to the floor I couldn't move nor could he. I walked to him finally very slowly and he headed to me without stretched arms I hugged him tightly and sobbed we stood there and cried out hearts out. I told him it was ok he kept sobbing "I tried to help him, I tried to help him and he went under fast" and that ended that. I told him there was no blame only sadness he had to go through this as I did.

We went to the funeral it was open casket he looked nice however had been I the water a long time.

He had his wedding ring on his Mom said she could not get that ring off for the funeral and was hostile about it actually. If she knew her son at all she would have known he would have wanted that ring on that finger no doubt. He loved his wife.

And suddenly she whirled and looked me straight in the face and very loudly said "and you were his girlfriend" just as loudly I responded "No, I was his friend" for God's sake I was approximately five years older than Ed and everyone in that room heard that conversation and no one liked her accusation at all. We were friends and good ones as I was with Kennedy. I walked away with my brother. He leaned over to me and said "well that was certainly impressive wasn't it?"

We sat through the service that was quite nice and then came time for the cemetery, several of the folks from the agency told me I was in no shape to go to the cemetery and said not to go. They knew I took Ed's death hard very hard as did Chris, my brother. I yielded and headed back to Pittsburg. Chris and I were mostly silent during that trip. By the time we got home we were ok and did talk very little. We were glad to be home.

I stayed with my brother for a while to be sure he was ok and then I went to my home. I shut and locked the door and commenced to cry my heart out for hours, till the next day.

I checked on Chris and started the day putting one foot in front of the other. Karl called to check in. I told him I was ok I would be fine and thanked him for caring. Hung up the phone and started my life completely alone, again.

I was doing fine at the new job. I was responsible for writing commercials, typing them up taking them to scheduling and typing for five salesmen. It was a busy job and quite a bit of responsibility but I loved it and was quite capable of the job. I was happy with my decision to leave Kansas City. Finally things were working out for me.

I learned a lot working for a TV station there were many things to learn. I seemed to lean heavily for the production end of things.

That is where my former training came in. I was good at direction and pretty good at the typing end of the commercial too. The station bought a new setup called the TK76. This was pretty much uptown equipment. It was a monitor which allowed you to do a commercial and see it playback instantly. It was a good selling point. When they put me in the sales department I sold that piece of equipment often. I loved production and had the pleasure of having people call the station asking who did thus and so commercial that would have been me. It was great fun and a real challenge.

I made some good friends at the station and laughed a lot. One of the fellas by the name of Mike was in the production end of things. We hit it off pretty well and his girlfriend Hanna was my good friend. Mike and Hanna decided to get married. Their wedding would take place in St George Mo. That was a five hour trip and we all worked till 10:30 so that would be a killer run literally but no one was about to give us any slack at all it had to be one way and I almost turned it down. That was pushing it and I don't push well as most people know. So I yielded to keep peace in the family which was against every fiber in my body. We made that run to St George and got there around 4 in the morning so we headed for the motel. We unloaded and all of us were in one room they had not cleaned the other room yet so here we are piled in one room exhausted and everyone was quick tempered me especially. I just lay down and tried to catch a nap if at all possible.

The fellas left and I was in a heap on the bed loving it. The door was thrown open and a person kind of fell into the middle of the room. I looked up and said "Polly, I presume" and the response was "do you know what it is like to come all this way with "Frick and Frack from Pittsburg?" Hence my meeting with Polly, Mikes sister. That meeting started over thirty years ago and is still going strong. We are actually getting close to 40 years of being best friends. What a meeting that was. We had a fantastic time at the wedding and we are still having a fantastic time with each other.

After we attended the wedding we headed home and we were back in the real world I was really wearing out on working two and three jobs just to make ends meet. The economy was really bad and everyone was feeling the hit. I didn't know what to do about it.

At this point in time I was working at the hospital as an aide, Home Care during the week, and at the mall in a little shop that sold a bit of everything. I was worn out with this schedule. Sometimes I went to another town 30 miles away and worked in that shop especially the sidewalk sales I loved to do them always did. They were a lot of work but I had a wonderful time meeting and greeting folks and selling I love to sell it was tremendous.

Polly and I remained friends throughout our entire lives we kept in touch no matter where we were.

Travelin Buddies

Polly and I always had a wonderful time with each other. She is an extremely intelligent individual and charismatic put that together and you have one hell of a wonderful relationship. I am older than Polly, I am older than anyone actually but we were a tremendous blend of humanity.

Polly does not travel well. Her bladder is the size of a nat. Yes, we spent a lot of time looking for bathrooms. One evening we went to Hepler, a very small town in the middle of nowhere we wanted to hear the band they were suppose to be quite good so we went. Coming back home Polly announced she had to pee in the middle of nothing in any directions not even any bushes.

I finally pulled of the road because she threatened to pee in the car. She got out of the car and walked about 15 steps and squatted. All at once a plane arrived with search lights and cars were coming in all directions it suddenly resembled LAX and there she was bare ass in the wind.

No matter where we went or what we did it was always funny and always a scene. When we first got to the place in Hepler that night we looked in the window knowing full well we looked like Japanese sunsets. But in we went and I heard a fella say to Polly, "well I sure know what you are" she paused, turned and faced him dead on and said "No worries darlin you sure can't afford me."

Polly had and still has a wicked sense of humor she is such fun and I needed her humor badly. We always have a good time always. No matter where we go we will get lost there is no doubt of that. This brings to mind one of our little side trips we took on a more serious note. It had been two or three months since Ed died and I wanted to go to his grave. I just had to go see his grave. I called Polly and told her to put on her pants we were going for a ride. Her response was "ok, where we going?" and my response was "St Joe". Polly realized that was where Ed was buried and it was time to go. I had to let go and this was the only way to do it.

We took off for on a 300 mile run due north. She asked me what the name of the cemetery was, I told her and where was it I said "I don't know. I have no idea." Somehow I drove straight to the cemetery and by that time it was quite dark and it was raining like God opened the gates of heaven and said "Let there be rain."

It was hard, loud heavy and very windy. I pulled in the cemetery and Polly looked at me and said "where is the grave?" I stopped the car, looked at her and said "I have no idea absolutely none but I will find it." She groaned as I stopped the car. She responded by saying "what are you doing?" and I said getting out and reading the little tombstones get out Polly and start reading. I will never forget that long heavy loud sigh as she slammed the door. There we were in a blinding rain looking for a grave that could have been anywhere. The lightning was snapping around us quick and horrifying close. I kept walking and all at once lightening came down dead ahead of me and the gravestone lit up with the lighting and there it was. I walked right to it in a matter of minutes. There was the grave of my very best friend that knew all my secrets and dreams. That was my buddy Ed. I remember screaming very loudly "I found him, I found him".

We headed home. I didn't say anything when we left the cemetery. I didn't talk for quite a while it was more than I could handle it really was. I thought a lot of him more than I realized. We headed back to Kansas City and found a motel and pulled in for the night. We would find a place to eat and go home the next day. We didn't have any night clothes so we slept in what we wore that was ok it wouldn't kill us it wasn't home sweet home it was somewhere to drop before we died.

This was a very hard day. I felt both relieved and pained. I found my buddy, Ed. "Good by my sweet sweet boy."

It seemed we drove forever. We stopped at Mickey D's and ate on the run. It seemed I had been driving all my life for some reason. We were thirty five miles from home and I looked to the right to see a lot of dust heading for the highway. It was a pickup and it was closing in fast. I started slowing down so as not to collide with that truck coming in like a bat out of hell. I watched with my mouth open the truck took a fast spin, and started rolling it vaulted into a field and flipped many many times. Then a dead stop. We sat and watched with open mouths. I pulled the car closer to see if there was life and there was. A lady got out of the car carrying a baby screaming loudly help me help me. I pulled the car into the field, told Polly to throw her into the back seat and she did so. She was holding her baby boy that looked to be about one year old. She screamed relentlessly, I turned the car around and headed to the closest hospital fast really fast I had that car floored. I was looking in the rear view mirror and all I could see was blood shooting in the air to the ceiling of the back seat. I told Polly to stop the bleeding with something if nothing else take off her shirt and apply pressure before the child bled to death.

She was screaming at me saying no I am not ripping my clothes off shut up and drive. And drive I did it scared her to death. We were going 100 with emergency lights on and my horn. That car was really hauling it up and down all of the hills and folks were pulling off the road thank God. I kept praying for a policeman to help but no, not a one. I thank God I was a good fast driver I was well in control unlike Polly I scared her to death.

We arrived at the hospital emergency got help instantly and then we got some rags and water to clean the car so the blood would not set. We finally got it clean.

We left the hospital when we found they were ok I wanted to go back to the scene. I wanted to get to the accident and get her purse knowing all of her identification would be there and that is important I knew that somehow.

Sure enough we found her purse and as I pulled it from the truck the police were coming in. They questioned us and that was fine I told them we were taking the id etc to the hospital because she would need it at the hospital. That officer looked at me and said "I am not believing this. Most folks would have kept going let along returning to get needed information for medical help" I responded by saying "this is logical to me at any rate." He shook my hand and we were on the way back to the hospital. We found the lady and she was ok a few scratches her boy had a huge cut down the middle of his skull but would be ok. She was pleased I had her id because she was not about to leave her boy. We knew everything was ok so we were out of there back "on the road again".

The rest of our trip was non eventful thank God I don't think we could have handled any more at all we were exhausted and so very thankful to see the house. God was so good!

Dare I Relocate One More Time?

I was in a quarry trying to decide if I wanted to stay in my home town and starve to death or relocate and go elsewhere and follow the money.

I was trying desperately to figure out what was the best to do stay or go this was so hard. I was so tired of relocating settling down and again uproot and move elsewhere. It seemed to be a pattern. Polly and I discussed this situation many many times and the answer was always the same relocate but where? I only had one option and that was Texas. I had a cousin there and could stay with her for a couple of weeks and get a job and a place to live. Mom told me they would arrange moving my things to Texas when I settled down in the meantime my brother could live in my house so it would not be vacant and keep the insurance in force. That sounded good but the relocating part. I just got home and really hated to leave I wanted to stay here.

But there was no way to do so. I had only been in my house three years and here I was one more time thinking of relocating again. Things had not been the greatest between Mom and me. Oftentimes it was really rocky and I could do without all that as could Dad I am sure. I wanted to stay but was tired of working so hard for nothing. I was also tired of the fighting endless bickering always.

I decided to go to Texas. The plan was pack personal possessions only and enough to get buy until I could settle somewhere. I had directions written down in the front seat $100 is all the money I had and was on the road.

I remember telling the folks good bye. Dad followed me in his car all the way out of town. I watched him turn off and wave good bye. That was a very sad time for me. I loved my Dad so much and we had been through so much.

We understood each other. All we had to do was to look at each other and we knew what the other one was thnking. It was amazing we were extremely close I always thanked God for that. I put the pedel to the metal and made good time. It was 7pm and I pulled into Dennison I didn't realize I was heading to Avon, I was always told they lived in Danford so I was concerned there was quite a discrepancy with the instructions here couldn't figure that out but went the way they instructions were stated. I was headed straight for Avon. I arrived at their house at 9 the next morning. I was glad to be there it was nerve racking to me going into the unknown and wondering why I was told Danford and written instructions were straight into Avon it was. amazing. I asked her why that was and the response was "no one knows where Danford is and everyone is familiar with Avon" So whatever, it didn't matter to me I made it to the destination and was certainly glad. When one drives you don't site see and now I could look around. I unpacked the car sor of and sat down. We discussed my immediate plans. I was staying there for approximately two weeks and would have a job I had no thought of not being able to work I had done a lot of things at the agency in Kansas City so I was ready. A fast typist can always work and I was fast very fast.

My cousin's husband worked for an insurance company at the time and they had an opening for a transcription typist. This is what I had done for several years and I knew insurance a very good handle on it. I went to the office and interviewed with his office manager and got the job. That was wonderful faster than I had anticipated actually so it was going very well.

I liked what I did there was a lot of insurance rating along with the transcription typing which was fine. I was to get paid every two weeks so when I my first check it would only be for one week because of holding it out till I got situated on timing as was the case in many jobs. Lots of companies did that and it was fine I knew that. However I did not get a check for thirty days and needless to say I was extremely broke by then. I had no money even for gas to get back and forth to work and that was silly there was no reason I didn't get my checks they had something screwed up bad and it was killing me. I didn't even have any lunch money for God's sake. I called the branch office and raised hell and did that twice. I got in hot water for that because I had no right to call them but no one else cared about my check but me that was apparent. I had every right to have a pay check by law.

That did not go over very well by then I didn't care at all I just wanted the money to move out and get another job end this damn story quick which is exactly what I did. As soon as they cut the check to shut me up I was out of there immediately turned in my notice and found another place to live other than their house. That was fine I appreciated the two weeks I stayed with them but the job sucked and I knew I certainly do much better and I was quite ready to do so.

I found an apartment a low rent type of place but it was not a career move I would not be there that long. I signed a six month lease that's all and I signed up with an agency and found a job all in the same week.

I found another job within a week for good money benefits etc The company was huge insurance company and I ran the CRT then and was in the workers comp division working for the adjusters.

I really got bored with that job rather quickly it was a no brainer and I needed more. I noticed they had an opening in their transcription department. They usually had two typists and were down to one so I told them I wanted to change departments. They had never heard of such a thing and couldn't imagine I was bored but they let me transfer. I loved it I typed all day long. I worked with a gal named Pat who became a lifelong friend. We were a tremendous team. They even closed down their typing pool in downtown Avon, claims division because we were fast enough to keep their departments up to minute and our own claims office too. We were fast really fast and it was a fun job.

In the mix of things I met a fella that lived in the same complex I moved into. We became good friends rather quickly actually. It was nice to have someone to visit with and go places with. It had been a very long time. We were buddies nothing more. His name was Jim.

We had fun together and I even went to church with him a couple of times and that was nice. Time flew by and we ended up going together as a couple and decided to get married. So we did. I knew it was a mistake the week after we made the fatal plunge. It was a huge mistake. Somehow we stayed married for 7 years and It was a struggle He was not abusive like before but suffocated me. He would not make any decision for himself. A great example of that would be he for some reason had to ask me what to wear for work every morning. Yes, every morning there were no decisions here he wore uniforms what is the huge difficulty?

Seriously. If I was going to the store to get bread he had to go and I as strong enough to carry a loaf of bread. This type of behavior was not flying well with me nope it surely wasn't. Then I became aware of lies he was a pathological liar about everything on this earth. He was not trustworthy at all. I had to hide money that was in the bank because if he knew we had $50 in the bank he would spend $100 so I learned the art of lying about the money and always putting in the wrong amount. I got to be quite good at that. Once in a while he had a meeting at night and that was wonderful I had a great evening with the dog and me. I loved it I would talk on the phone or whatever, I felt free and enjoyed that time alone I really did.

Then on top of this, I knew if I said anything about a divorce Mom would again throw it up in my face "I told you so"

I wanted to visit with someone but there was no one there actually so there I was again way out on the limb and that became my home for a rather long time. My folks were really strange about some things. I remember after we got married and the Thanksgiving holiday rolled around and we had the time off I called Mom and said "guess who is coming home for dinner Thanksgiving?" Her response was "I don't remember asking you" so that ended that. We stayed home. I was crushed but said nothing to no one just like always. I think what really got to me was one year Thanksgiving came up and I was planning on coming home for the holidays like always. I always liked to go home and spend time with the folks.

Mom called and told me she was not having Thanksgiving that year my brother was in the midwest on a roundup herding cattle to and from someplace so he would not make it and Mom didn't want to have a big dinner without him.

I understood that, well kinda. My feelings were hurt but I did understand I guess. Thanksgiving day came and I called home to wish them Happy Thanksgiving and my brother answered the phone. I was floored I was glad to visit with him and I asked what they had for dinner and he said "turkey, dressing, mashed pot…" and the list went on and on. That was a no brainer for me to put together you do not fix that big of a meal without a warning. It has to be planned out. I know I have done it many many times. Mom took the phone and back peddling fast.

I didn't make a big deal out of it what was done it was done move on….I always had the feeling she was glad I was in Texas out of sight out of mind sort of thing. Maybe I was wrong but I didn't think so. Sometimes I would think back about the days at the School that I loved so much and the friends that I thought so much of. I kept track sometimes without them knowing of course. The one that I was always wondering about was Eric Lawson the one true love of my life. One night in particular I called one of my buddies, and he freaked and was so happy to hear from me and it was fantastic to talk with him. I asked him about our other buddy and they were fine. I hung up and the phone rang it was Joe. God Bless Joe Evans he was a really good buddy. Joe and John C were both from New York both very talented beyond belief and I adored both of them. That was a wonderful evening and I could hardly wait for Jim to come home because I had fantastic news. I found my friends, well two of them anyway. He finally got home and I told him I visited with Johnny and Joe from the playhouse.

They were both living in Hollywood and doing extremely well.

John C was set designer and Joe did backgrounds for movies one was for one of the greatest ever filmed. They were doing extremely well. Jim's mouth fell open and he said "you really know these folks?" I laughed and said "of course, I went to school with them and we were really good buddies." That phone call really made me feel warm and fuzzy. It brought back fantastic memories that has kept me going for many years.

The next evening Joe called me and invited me to come visit for a few days, I couldn't believe it I said yes of course. I made plans for Thursday and returning on Sunday. That was long enough to visit and have hours to catch up. I asked if I could bring a good friend of mine which of course would have been Pat and he agreed by saying '" am holding the door open sweetheart."

I can't describe how happy I was that night there are no words it was like going home it was a fantastic feeling. I called Pat and we made arrangements and we were like two school girls going on a first date.

It was fantastic absolutely fantastic. She was so excited to finally meet the other part of my life that had been so fractured. Joe lived in Hollywood right down the street about a mile from Universal Studio. We got in late and he picked us up I was looking for him in the airport and Pat was looking for luggage I spotted him and screamed clear across the airport and we made a beeline run toward each other it was a dream come true. We were so busy hugging each other it was like a movie. He poured us in the car and away we went. He drove and drove and drove. Pat leaned up in the seat and said "Joe where are we now" He sighed and said "the airport" and we all laughed till our sides split …. We got home, ate a wonderful meal they had prepared then we went to bed. Pat took a deep breath and said "here I am in Hollywood California and Bob Hope lives two doors down, who would have known"

Joe threw together a fantastic party for me he invited about 20 people that I knew well and they were all so pleased to see me and I them. It was a fantastic evening one I will never forget. Joe was up at the crack of dawn cooking for the evening God love this man he is Golden. People started coming that evening and Pat was floored they were mostly in the movies TV production end of things names she heard of

such as John C set designer he won an Emmy in the 90's for a show called Dina. And of course Joe, Henry Carson that was in the TV series Henry, Nan who did voices for Disney films and the story goes on. I leaned back in the chair and whispered to her

"Pat if you want to go to bed don't hesitate go ahead I know you are tired I am so you go ahead if you wish there is no problem" She looked at me and said "I have never seen people like this in my life and will never again have the opportunity I don't want to miss one single thing" That made me feel so good.

That night was Golden it really was till this day. The memories of that night I hold dearly and always will. Pat passed away last year and that even makes this more special. I gave my best buddy a night to remember. I did manage to make a phone call to CBS to see if per chance Eric was there. He was on vacation and not returning until the next day when we were leaving. My heart was pounding so hard I held my breath. His secretary said I could leave him a message and she would be sure to get it. I told her I was an old friend from the School days. I left my name and office number. I knew he would call I knew he would.

Our time in Hollywood was over too soon and we headed back to transcription and our insurance company jobs.

We were exhausted and very pleased with the fun we had it was so nice. Pat was so glad she had gone with me.

We went back to work on Monday. We pounded the keys with electric IBM typewriters and worked them to death. I did that for three years and became bored with that also. It was time to go and Pat was looking too. We were done. We both decided it was time to move,

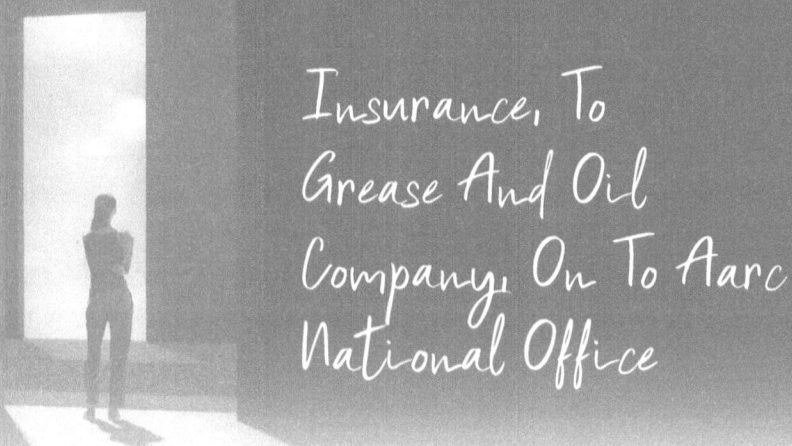

Insurance, To Grease And Oil Company, On To Aarc National Office

I found a job working for a grease and oil company funded through the United Kingdom typical secretarial position I was in the communication department again dictation typing. There I learned how to use the Lexitron one of the first computer types of equipment I informed my supervisor I was out typing the gal on the Lexitron by half and had no machine. I wanted that machine it fascinated me I told my supervisor if she gave me the machine for a week I could way out type anyone in the office. She did and so did I. I loved that machine and could really type like lightening it was wonderful.

    I met that challenge mastered it and was ready for much much more. I applied for another job at the AARC national office in Dallas. I applied on my lunch hour. I interviewed and one week later I had the job. Full benefit package and I was responsible for building the education department. That was really a good job and I had never had many benefits since I left the agency in the City. My job consisted of taking all of the paperwork out of the filing cabinets into the computer. The turned me loose and so began the Education Department for the United States. It was a load and I accepted it well. It was a wonderful job with a lot of inventory to work with. I was having a really good time setting up the systems that worked with great tracking systems. Computers have always fascinated me and they still do. I love to learn what they will do.

Pat never was particularly taken with computers they made her nervous and she never wanted to learn anything more than what she needed.

As it worked out, there was an opening at AARC where I worked it was in the membership department. I knew she could do that job and the only thing holding her back was no computer knowledge. It was good start up pay and again fantastic benefits. Pat was divorced with a little girl with her so benefits were very important as was salary. I told her of the job in detail and also the computer. She balked because of the computer. I promised her I would teach her every step of the way. I said "Pat you trust me" and she did.

After she interviewed they asked me about her and I told them she was the best employee they could possibly have ever. They hired her and found I was correct. She was a good worker too. I taught her the computer enough to get by and call me if she got stuck and I would bail her out. That is how we worked it and I managed to cover her very well. We were always a good team and this was no different. Thank God I could teach her. Pat remained at that for around 25 years so it was a perfect fit absolutely perfect.

Unfortunately for me they hired a Director of Education and I clashed with him no matter what I did. I tried very hard to get along with him and this did not work no way.

One day he came to my desk with a book that had been returned that I had sent somewhere. He threw it at me for the wrong address. I pulled the information on their stationery was the very same as where I sent it. I showed it to him and he said "I cannot nor will I accept that as an answer". So there it was handwriting on the wall I was out of there. I knew I could get a job I was good worker and fantastic typist so that was a mute point. His superior told me she would give me a great reference without any problem she knew the problem so… there I was again.

This was rugged finding a job at that time in Texas. You were either a Texan or you would not work, so that took some time till it settled down again. I filed for unemployment so was ok actually.

In between these jobs I filed for divorce I could not handle moving all the time and telling a gown man what to wear to work when he always wore a uniform. I was there seven years and that was all I could deal with. It did not work I was a workaholic and he was lazy, a liar etc. I think the crowning glory came when I got back from Texas. When I left I gave Jim all the bills to be paid checks were in envelopes all he had to do was to put them in the mailbox on the way to his job. WRONG when they came due again I discovered he paid a different amount. He changed everything after I left so he would have more money. I could not trust him with anything and was worn out with all this and refused to keep going in a marriage that was a façade name only I was done completely done.

It is amazing how our lives change so fast, everything changes like lightening. Here I was looking at the second divorce what was wrong with me? Why did all this keep happening?

I was getting numb to the whole thing. I told him I was finished and there was no choice in the matter at all.

In one week I moved, bought a different car, filed for divorce, I had a hysterectomy, which was a really busy week. I was certainly ready for a huge break I really was. In spite of it all I felt like the weight of the world was lifted from me. Then one evening around 6 the phone rang. It was none other than Eric Lawson I never thought I would hear his voice again ever. I began to feel as though he was nothing more than imaginary my God he was real, at the other end of the phone. I started crying that's all I could do and it sounded like he was having trouble too. He called to invite me to the School reunion.

He would pick me up and I could stay with them till I was ready to leave he begged me to come I took a deep breath and said "yes, I would love to". And so there it was it was still there whatever it was I would come in on Thursday and return home to Dallas the following Sunday evening. I was on cloud nine I really was on cloud nine. It had been 27 years of waiting as he stated. It was a very long wait. 27 years we were both so excited I could not imagine we would have a weekend together He was married but that's ok I would see him, be with him talk to him explain to him and above all somehow tell him I still love him I would have to find the words and I was weak in that area I never said that to any one before never. The reason for that is I never loved anyone but him and I didn't want to waste the words on someone else. Those words meant something to me. He waited a long time to hear me say that a very long time. I was to take a cab to the hotel and he would pick me up there. I did as I was told.

I sat there and yes he was early. I saw him come around the corner and ran into his open arms I waited 27 years for that hug 27 years. It was beautiful. We were so happy to see each other. It was written all over us we could see it on each other. He put me in the car and we sat there and stared at each other. Whoever said love never dies was correct I can tell you that first hand and so could he.

After the initial shock we started chatting non stop as he drove. He wanted to know everything absolutely everything. What happened to us and I told him everything he was in shock and had no idea what happened to me absolutely no clue. He was visibly shaken when he heard what happened about the burning of everything etc etc and going to the doctor that was humiliating and even humiliating to talk about.

We got to the house, unloaded me from the car and went in to meet his wife. She was very very nice, fun and welcoming. They were evenly matched and I was glad. He said they were ok.

He went on to say it was a marriage of convenience for both of them. Nuff said. One night he took me to work with him. She had never been there and I couldn't believe it. He was a director at CBS in Hollywood I loved it. I definitely knew my way around a TV station. He was showing me that station and introducing me to everyone and there was a huge tremor he asked if I would pull the wire and I said you bet so there we were working together at CBS in Hollywood. What a wonderful night, absolutely wonderful. He even let me sit in on their meeting they had so I could hear things they were doing. I understood all of it they even asked my opinion on a couple of things and I took the floor stating why I thought what I did and they agreed with me.

That was amazing. Eric was so proud of me that night. His wife was very very quiet and shy unlike me.

Saturday night was the reunion it started early and on into the night. Started getting ready and his wife said she wasn't going I freaked because I assumed she would be going I never thought otherwise. I tried to get her to go but she was not going. She said she knew no one and it was silly we should go together. He didn't argue with her. He smiled and said ok done deal we can handle it. And yes we could thank you God. I guess I should have felt bad but I didn't I was so glad after the fact it was a sin. I have to say we had a great time every one was there that we knew, it was fantastic. Many commented that it was good to see us together and I can say it was wonderful we were together it felt as though we belonged together just like it felt 27 years prior. What a night what a fantastic afternoon and evening it was no way would I trade it no way on this earth.

We talked a lot on the way home he told me he knew in his heart I would surface. He said "we meant to much to each other for you never to return." I told him for the first time that I did in fact love him then, when separated and now, my feelings never at any point ever changed. He admitted the same for him that felt so good to me it really did. He told me we should be together and there is no denying that at all. And then we were home. I had one more day with him the next day I headed home I didn't want any of this to end I really didn't. God forgive me "if this is wrong, I don't want to be right" The next day we didn't do much Violet had to work so she was gone all day. We went out to eat in the evening, the next day I left. It was a nice sunny day and we went for a walk around the area it was a fantastic day. We chatted with the neighbors and he introduced me to everyone we met. He asked if I wanted lunch and no way could I eat and he couldn't either. I packed, got ready to go and we headed for the airport. We didn't say much in the car it was sad I shed a few tear very quietly.

We got to the airport and he carried the suitcase and held my hand. We stopped at the gate and looked at each other. He kissed me good bye and it felt more like hello. He hugged me so tight I couldn't breathe. He whispered dear God don't go please don't go not again. I said "I don't want to go, I have to go I want to stay right here with you forever" We kissed one more time as they said last time to board. We looked at each other for a long long time. We knew it would be the last time. And so it was, he passed away in 2006. I said good bye to the only man I ever really loved. I thank God for the opportunity.

I returned to Dallas and got a Divorce. I talked with Eric again on the phone and then I told him I was divorced and he said "my God why didn't you tell me? You never said a word" my response was "I didn't dare Eric I would have stayed with you and what a mess we would have had, both of us" his response was "I guess you were right, what would I have done with Violet? It's a good thing one of us had some sense" We talked off and on for the next year. He wanted me to return badly but I didn't I sayed in Dallas unfortunately. I always wanted to return that too was a dream that was never realized.

Private Investigator

Things were going well and at a fast pace. It had been five years since I got a divorce and was doing very well. That was fine with me I was ready to settle down and get a life like a real person. The job I was told about was working for a private investigator in Texas suburb of Dallas. That's ok I had a place to live in Irving so things were really looking up. The money was decent the draw back was I had to pay the agency that found the job for me. Something told me to take the job and I did. It did not matter if I was paying them for the job it was worth it. I had an opportunity to really move in that place. The handwriting was on the wall The owner had a wonderful idea but no idea in the world of how to pull it off. I did. I knew how to do it.

    I worked for this man one week and decided where to start. I worked with the 4 other typists that were part time. And they were really part time there was no doubt about that. I could not work without any semblance of order to it so I started in with my own system at my desk. I have to find things or I can't work. Or not efficient at any rate. I just kept organizing and one day we had a meeting in the owners office. We were all called in. We sat down and he looked at me for some reason and said "tell me what the problem is in word processing" my response was "do you really want to know or are you just askin" he said at that point he was interested in really knowing what took so long to get the work done.

    I told him we needed a new computer and printer for starter. After the meeting we went to lunch. When we returned I had a printer and new computer sitting on my desk. I was thrilled to death. I went to his office and thanked him so much. He looked at me and said "ok. You got the printer and the computer now missey make me money."

Two days later he made me the supervisor of the department and it was straight up from there. Instead of only 70 reports a month coming from word processing we have 780 which was more like it. I set up a complete system. He didn't want to spend money so instead of buying all of the file folders we turn them inside out and erased the names and wrote over the labels.

We saved a ton of money that way and all the work was really rolling out well. It went so well he told me later that other firms used my ideas to organize their own offices nationwide. I was very pleased at that I worked very hard to build it and it paid off for everyone. We all made money especially the owner and that was as it should be. That was the best job I ever had. The agency grew to nationwide in a short amount of time. It truly grew too fast actually. I have always felt that job was my favorite because the mission was to expose fraud in the workplace. We burned the folks taking advantage of Workers Compensation. It was for a wonderfully good cause. I hated the idea of someone collecting comp that lied to get it so we "burned" them as it should be. Everything was working well using my systems. The boss gave me a $5,000 raise which certainly told me he was satisfied with my work. I know for a fact the outside clients were very well pleased they could check on a client and have an

answer in approximately 30 seconds compared to a week before I started. This was good and running like a well oiled machine.

Things were really going every well for me finally. It went so well that the agency that I was paying for this tremendous job called and told me I was paid in full because I never missed a payment and was good for the contract. Therefore, I was paid in full. That was truly a blessing. That was fantastic because I was paying them $200 per month so that was like a raise.

We did have a great system and everyone did very well with the system and how it worked. Every now and then they got upset with me and reported me to the boss for something and we would have a meeting.

I remember they were all upset with me for some reason and the boss said "I don't care if she wants to run this like the U S Military just shut up and do it. She is doing her job when are you going to start doing yours?"

I had good back up I certainly did. It was a good job and lots to do always I taught them how to present things and not to assume things. I had spent several years working on the compensation side of insurance and knew **it** well. My knowledge paid off nicely. I enjoyed teaching them what to do and what not to do there is a lot of legality on things that you have to be familiar with leave no loop holes that is important.

It was a job that you learned every day about something and I loved that part of the job. For some unknown reason the gals thought it important that I dated. There was a lot of concern about that. Really they were thinking it would take some of the heat off of them if I was interested in a male companion. They could not understand I was not interested in anything except my job and I loved it. I wanted my boss to do well I had a lot of my time vested in his office, I really cared about it.

One say I was sitting in my office working on something and one of the girls brought in a fella to introduce me to him. This was a very good friend of hers that she had known for years and as it worked out he was divorced. Well figure this out it took ten seconds. I at first wanted to reach over and slap her but then I found it amusing. She was trying to help me out. I didn't need any help but I played the game and accepted her "help" as it were. Enter into my life Carson Grant.

He was ok as men go I guess. Actually he was a lot of fun. He asked me out for lunch and also for the coming Saturday night he wanted to go out. So here I was going out pleasing everyone. Carson was fun and he was quite intelligent which was enlightng to me at least.

We did have a good time we laughed a lot. He was quite intelligent and that was a plus a huge plus for once. Whatever we had a good time If he wanted to go out I would go and enjoy myself no doubt.

We ended up going together for eight years and of course the folks did not like him either. Ah such is life right?

We ended up getting married. We were doing ok actually. He had a really good job with Aetna Insurance Co at the claims office in down town Dallas. I was working temp for a stock broker in Ft Worth. We were doing okay for a while at least.

We did quite well actually until Aetna claims pulled out of Dallas and Carson had a choice to move to New Orleans or Connecticut. I was saying no to both areas one was really a depressed area and the other was expensive beyond belief and winters ungodly so...

In the mix of things I got a phone call, my brother was in intensive cre dying and I was called home. I got out of Texas so fast it was unreal. I was sitting in the plane thinking this wlll never happen again I am too far away, this will never happen again. I literally prayed all the way home. I made it to the hospital. He was in a coma but, he did know I was there. It was a day from hell. I was gravely worried about the folks with this. They had been through a lot and were getting up in years. My brother Chris was the favorite chid and always had been. Mom never really understood me but she and Chris were close really close as it is in most famlies. I was more like my Dad in all areas. Chris was the glue and I seemed to just be there which was ok, I was use to it actually.

I was there with the folks for several hours. I was so thankful I was there when he passed away. Like it or not they needed me and I was there as it should be.

It was a horrific day. He was at the house with Mom and suddenly gurgled and was pretty much out. It was a cardiac infraction. He was dead when he hit the floor. Mom was there by herself, Dad had gone to the grocery store to get something for them. She screamed when he came back, the EMT was there and the rest is history. It was fast really fast thank God. Everyone was in shock and I was never as tuned in as I was then. I thought a lot of my brother we were quite close. We had 17 years between us but it didn't seem like that much. We had a good relationship really good.

We all remained until the end which was at 7:30 that night. That horrible horrible night.

I got the folks home and situated somehow. Mom was destroyed Dad and I were In shock but there we were. Somehow we were ok if you want to call it that. He had been through a lot for 37 years of age. He had been a heavy drugger, dried out from that and also alcohol. Then he was running and hit a curb with his ankle and it ruined his ankle the bones were powder and nothing left of bone to set and fix. He had trouble with it the rest of his life. I was such a shame all he went through cold turkey and have that happen to him which disabled him for life.

The next day was hell it was time for the funeral arrangements, etc and I was to write the obituary which tore me apart. I never in this lifetime thought I would be writing my brother's obituary for the paper. It was a horrible day.

Mom went off. I remember her saying "well everything has ended it is a ll gone. There will be no more Christmas, Thanksgiving, Anniversary or any other holidays it is over all over. There will be no more ever again"

At that juncture Dad told her she also "had a daughter sitting on the couch in plain site." You know that was common however. On the holidays there were many photos of my brother as a youngster sitting on Santa's knee etc. His pictures were all over the house and never a photo of me. I never understood that it was like I didn't exist at all for anything. One time my brother asked me about that. He noticed it and I told him that was the way it was. He looked at me and said "I can't imagine why you don't hate me" my response was, "hey not your fault I have always loved you and you are well aware of it and that is all that is important". I will never forget that, ever. I remember I would look up and pray for wisdom that is all I could do and I did that often. It was hard very hard.

Time came for me to go home to Dallas and I told Carson I needed to return to my home. The folks needed me and I needed to be there for them.

I immediately started getting things in order for a move home. It was hard to do very hard to do. I had a type of a life in Texas and that ended abruptly as it should have. This had to be rather fast.

I talked with Carson he knew the situation and seemed to accept it as a done deal. He had no problem go to my hometown he said that was the thing to do. He was very cooperative and quite willing to help any way he could. I was surprised in one way and yet I wasn't. It was strange very strange.

I would be moving ahead of Carson. I would move January and he would bring the furniture in February. That way I would have time to find a job and a place to live before he came with the rest of things.

The time came and moving was happening. I was sad and happy at the same time. I found a house to rent and a job so my end was going very smooth which was surprising. We talked quite often on the phone so we had contact and we each knew what we were doing. The time went pretty fast actually and the physical move itself was smooth from the truck to the house.

This Thing Called Life

So we set up our house and started living somewhat. Carson was looking for work and since he was divorced previously he was going to contact the legal department and see what he had to do to get the hild support lowered. At the time of his previous divorce it was set rather high due to the fact he was making good money. He was sending $500 per month which was steep. That was his mission and quite capable of being lowered. He knew that. We each had their jobs to do his was lower child support and me a job. That was the plan. All of this happened in February.

Time marched on as they say. The folks never spoke to him or allowed him into their house at all. He never stopped me from going to visit the folks which I did at least once a week. That is the way it was. It worked however this was not ideal, I still couldn't understand why we could not be normal I gave up and handled it like I handled everything else.

For some unknown reason I walked off the porch and broke my ankle which was an unwanted distraction but there is was. I have always been graceful and one more time my grace and poise caught up with me. Carson was not home that time of course but I somehow managed to get on the porch and info the front room to the couch and prop my ankle up. I was a mess and he was not pleased at all. After two or three hours and my foot swelling up to extra large he decided he better take me to the hospital. They checked the information they had on me and they had emergency contact as my father. I was in no mood to change the information I was racked in pain at that point and let it go it was unimportant to me. I was taken care of and they put me in a cast. It was a clean break which was a miracle it broke and set itself exactly where it needed to be. So that took care of me for six weeks. Missing work for a while and I hated that we needed the money. Carson could not find a job he had been trying since February and could not come up with anything.

One day when the mail came with a renewal notice for his truck and the plates from Texas. He renewed it and things went ding ding. Before I broke my ankle I told him I knew something was wrong and he should have had a job and he had not done the legal things to lower his child support. I was sole support and was not happy. Then I broke my ankle. I was out of the cast July 20. I remained with Carson for 8 years and then we got married. Our life was ok he was good to me and we had a lot in common. We went to junk yards on Saturday often we enjoyed doing that for some reason. We were always looking for mirrors for his car, cigarette lighters etc literally junk as the name implies.

Since I knew insurance and was a really good transcription typist I decided to go into a free lance business typing "statements" for insurance companies. A "statement" is when the adjuster visits with the insured and records the interview and the transcription becomes a matter of record. I had done that sort of thing for years and decided I would do it on my own and make money on the side as a supplement. I did that and it grew a lot. I worked full time, came home and typed till way late at night. For me it was easy work. Carson did the spell check on the machine for the finish. In a very short time I increased to making $3,000 per week which was quite a jump to say the least. It was wonderful. Now here is where my trust killed me. In all the time and money I never saw any of it. You read that correct, I saw no money and was really making a small fortune at the time. I never questioned anything I just typed and made money and Carson handled the bank accounts. He did that so well I had no problem with the setup we had and I had complete blind trust in him. Why wouldn't I my own husband right? WRONG as I said I did not see one penny from all the typing. I needed help with the typing had a friend type with me and she messed up the entire account by erasing the tapes totally. That cost me a lot but nothing I could do about it. I was way too trusting but I learned finally. Never trust anyone and I don't to this day so I did learn and I assume that is ok. It was a hard lesson for me to learn. It was a good thing when he left me actually. We spent eight years together and were married for one year and it was over. I hate to admit it but it was the best thing that happened to me, being left as I was. I will admit that. To this day I have absolutely no idea where the money went but I am assuming it was a nice nest egg for Carson when he did leave me. He told me he was going back to Texas. I was not surprised, I asked when and he responded "Saturday" it was Wednesday then. I knew it was going to happen I waited on it actually.

I am use to feeling what is going on. It seems he was really irate when he took me to the hospital and they had my Dad as emergency contact not him. I told him I didn't know how they had the information at all because I had never been to that hospital in my life which was true.

That is what pulled the trigger. If that is all it took I told him to pack. So here I am again. As a very dear friend said to me once "I have worn out two perfectly good guardian angels and the third one was really weak"

This was not the only thing however. He owned up to the fact he never tried to get the child support down. He went on to say he neglected to tell me he owed the IRS $50,000. I told him I would file for divorce and he could come in October to sign the papers or at least read the decree and sign later. Under no circumstances did he want a divorce. Well of course he didn't that way the law could collect off me because I was married to him and he wasn't working. At that juncture I knew why he wanted to get married. I could not believe it I have to be the most stupid individual God ever made but He does take care of fools so I was obviously in the correct line.

Carson took off for Texas as planned and I moved as planned. I moved in with my girlfiend which was just fine. We loved each other and it worked well. God bless Ann, I don't know what I would have done without her no way could I do all this without her moral support. We worked together in Home Health Care years earlier. She was a blessing to me. I must say this. In the very beginning I told Carson one day I would come home from work and I would find a note pinned to the chair, "sorry I am gone, thanks for everything". He laughed, I didn't funny it almost came down to that didn't it?

I called Mom and asked her to go to lunch with me. She said yes and also knew I wanted to talk. I told her I was divorcing Carson he had already left for Texas. She asked me if I wasn't just copping out on the wedding vows.

I told her about the $50,000 and the other things and that settled her down before it started. Thank God she was not causing me grief with this no way was she. I was supporting him and it was coming to an end. Quickly.

Carson as promised showed up in October and again in November. That was the end of the entire thing Thanksgiving it was all over. He was not happy but that was the way it was. It was not right there was nothing about it right but it was done. Completely finished. Did I feel bad? NO I did not, it was the thing to do because I had to survive. I did everything I knew to do he is the one that would not go to job interviews. He did not want to get a job and be entrenched here in a small town. I was broken hearted not because of his leaving, but he took the dream of ever having a marriage that mattered away from me. There would never be a person that mattered in my life. The only one that ever really mattered to me at all was always Eric Lawson. No one else.

I had a decent job, place to live, was in my home town…God was good to me. He always opened that other door always.

He made it so that I was here for my Dad when he died. I was here for his last words. I was here for Mom's last words, I was here for Chris. I was where I was suppose to be. I was always where I was suppose to be.

No matter what happened in this family my love of family was never, ever faded or jaded I loved every one of them with a fierce love as I did Karl, Ed, Saundra and Eric. God bless them all. It seemed Carson was merely the vehicle to the ending.

www.ingramcontent.com/pod-product-compliance
Lightning Source LLC
Chambersburg PA
CBHW021427070526
44577CB00001B/102